ABSOLUTE
SURRENDER

ABSOLUTE SURRENDER

ANDREW MURRAY

BRIDGE
LOGOS
FOUNDATION

Alachua, Florida 32615

Bridge-Logos
Alachua, FL 32615 USA

Absolute Surrender
by Andrew Murray

Printed in the United States of America.

Library of Congress Catalog Card Number: 2007924138
International Standard Book Number: 978-0-88270-028-1

Contents

*O*ne day I was talking with a missionary and he said to me, "Brother, remember that when God puts a desire into your heart, He will fulfill it."

That helped me; I thought of it a hundred times. I want to say the same to you who are plunging about and struggling in the quagmire of helplessness and doubt. The desire that God puts into your heart, He will fulfill.

If any are saying that God has no place for them, let them trust God and wait, and He will help them and show them their place. I have learnt to place myself before God every day, as a vessel to be filled with His Holy Spirit. He has filled me with the blessed assurance that He, as the everlasting God, has guaranteed His work in me. If there is one lesson that I am learning day by day, it is this: that it is God who worketh all in all. Oh, that I could help any brother or sister to realize this!

Andrew Murray

Biography of Andrew Murray

*D*uring the nineteenth century, a number of church revivals swept the world and brought many to Christ who would otherwise never have found Him. In the Dutch Reformed Church of South Africa such a revival occurred in the last half of the 1800s. One man stands out as a principal force behind that movement. His name was Andrew Murray. And fortunately for us, not only was he a great preacher and evangelist, he was also a great writer.

Andrew was born in South Africa in 1828. His father and mother were missionaries with the Dutch Reformed Church, having originally emigrated from Scotland. Eventually his father became pastor of a South African church, raising his children in godly fashion, with regular family prayer and hymn singing in the home.

At that time, the first great Christian revival was beginning to move. Andrew's father prayed often for revival to come to his church. Every Friday evening he read to his family accounts of great movements of the Holy Spirit throughout the history of the Church. Then he retired to his study to pray, pouring his heart out in tears, pleading with God for a similar outpouring of the Holy Spirit in South Africa.

When Andrew was ten, he and his older brother John were sent to school in Aberdeen, Scotland. There they stayed with their paternal uncle, a well-known minister associated with the Free Church. Their uncle, like their father, was highly interested in the growing revival movement. But unlike South Africa, Scotland was experiencing a series of revivals similar to those taking place in America during the Great Awakening (1795-1835) under Charles Grandison Finney.

Andrew and his brother found themselves in the hub of the movement. Because of his association with the Free Church and his interest in revival, Andrew's uncle frequently had as houseguests the great evangelists and preachers of the day. The young Murray brothers were enthralled by lively conversations on the revival movement and its commitment to a deeper spiritual life.

Close association with men and women of strong faith and intimate knowledge of what God was doing throughout Scotland and America led to the brothers' collective decision to enter the ministry, much to the delight of their uncle and their parents back home in South Africa. So in 1845 the Murray brothers left Scotland for Holland to begin theological studies at the University of Utrecht. Andrew was seventeen at the time.

While in school Andrew made a trip to Germany to see Pastor John Blumhart, who conducted a ministry of healing the sick and casting out demons. Blumhart attributed his success to nothing less than the "experience of the real presence of the Lord Jesus." As he witnessed the healings, Andrew realized that greater power was available to the Church than most Christians realized.

Ironically and in sharp contrast, however, church life in Holland varied from lukewarm to cold. One professor at the university even taught that there are no such things as miracles, that everything could be explained by scientific and natural laws. This way of thinking was part of a new rationalism and formalism that was taking over the Dutch church. But Andrew had already witnessed the miraculous power of God in action. He knew that rationalism and formalism were wrong, and began to seriously question the instruction he was getting at the university.

Fortunately for their growing spiritual life, John and Andrew found a fellowship at the university patterned after the discipleship societies of John Wesley. It was called Zechar Debar (Hebrew for "Remember the Word"). The fellowship worked as a system of "checks and balances" for the brothers. No matter what was taught in the classroom, the Murrays' association with this group kept them steadfast and committed to the orthodox biblical theology they had received in South Africa and Scotland.

Disagreement with and departure from classroom theology aside, Andrew came to a deeper realization that he truly belonged to the Lord. He later referred to this as his "conversion." He was also ordained by the Dutch Reformed Church after he completed his studies at the age of twenty, the youngest ever to do so.

Following his ordination, he returned to South Africa and was assigned to a small church in the frontier town of Bloemfontein. Covering about 50,000 square miles, his parish had a sparsely scattered population of only 20,000, most of whom were farmers. These Dutch colonists (Boers) had a reputation for fierce independence, and were not easily impressed by outsiders. But even at the age of twenty-one, Andrew so impressed his congregation with his concern and earnest desire to help their families both spiritually and educationally that he was an almost immediate success.

In 1854 he traveled to England on church business. He had been reluctant to leave his parish, but because he had developed a worsening problem with pain in his arms and hands, he decided to leave for a while in order to regain his health. Unfortunately, the rest did not cure his problem, and he had recurrent symptoms throughout the rest of his life.

But the trip was not a complete failure. On his way home he stopped at Cape Town to visit some friends. Originally planning to stay only a few days with them, he changed his mind when he met their daughter Emma. After extending his stay two more weeks, he proposed to her. She turned him down. But Andrew was in love and persistent. He wooed her through letters and several return trips to win her heart. Eventually, she accepted his proposal. They were married in Cape Town on July 2, 1856. Andrew was twenty-eight and Emma was twenty-one.

Emma was a perfect complement to Andrew. She was schooled in music, art, and languages, was widely read, spiritual, pious and social. She would become adept at managing their soon-to-be large and bustling household. The Murrays reared eight children: four sons and four daughters. Not the least of Emma's talents was serving as a buffer between Andrew and all those who would monopolize his time, taking him away from his family and

4

necessary time with God.

Emma also helped Andrew in his work. When he could not write because of the chronic pain in his hands and arms, she took dictation. She also developed many ministries of her own—helping women and their families in need, starting prayer groups, and creating activities for the children of the congregation in support of missionary work. Supporting Andrew, she enjoined his battles against church leaders in Cape Town over the creeping liberalism that was working its way into the Reformed Church.

Interestingly, when revival finally came to his church, Murray resisted it. At first glance, this is difficult to understand. After all, he had grown up in the house of a father who prayed passionately for revival and the house of an uncle who facilitated it and exposed young Andrew to the finest minds of the movement. Murray, himself, had prayed for revival. But when the time came for him to participate, he was held back by his belief that the Holy Spirit only moved through the preaching of the Word, and, therefore, only through the pastor. He felt unworthy.

He expressed his personal concern in a letter to one of his friends:

> *When I look at my people, my peace forsakes me. I am forced to flee to the Master to seek a new and more entire surrender to His work. My prayer is for revival, but I am held back by the increasing sense of my own unfitness for the work. I lament the awful pride and self-complacency that have now ruled my heart. Oh, that I may be more and more a minister of the Spirit.*

In spite of Murray's personal misgivings, he would not avoid revival for long. Shortly after moving to the geographically smaller and more urban parish of Worchester in 1860, he was introduced to the revival movement in a highly dramatic fashion.

In recounting the event, an associate reported that Murray was finishing a sermon when one of the church elders came running into the sanctuary to tell him that there was a great commotion in the nearby youth meeting hall. Apparently, he reported, a young native girl, standing in the back of the hall during prayer time, had asked if she could share a hymn and pray. Within a short time she was on her knees praying loudly, and soon others in the room joined her in spontaneous song and prayer.

Murray followed his friend to investigate. As they neared the room, the sound grew louder and louder. Murray, confused by the thunderous noise he couldn't identify, opened the door and discovered that all sixty young people were on their knees loudly praying and praising God. They didn't notice their pastor when he entered the room. Deciding that this behavior was inappropriate, he tried to silence them, but they didn't hear him. They continued praying and singing late into the night, finally leaving the church to go out into the streets where others joined them.

At the next church meeting, Murray finished his sermon. As he led everyone in prayer, the members of the congregation—young and old—spontaneously and simultaneously knelt and loudly prayed their own prayers. Again he tried to quiet them, walking up and down the aisle, begging his flock to calm down. But this time a stranger in the back of the church interrupted him, telling the preacher that he had just come from America where he had witnessed the very same thing happening. He told Andrew that he needed to realize that the Spirit of God was at work in his church and that he should do nothing to stop it.

At that moment, the pastor underwent a transformation. He realized that in spite of him, the revival he had been praying for had finally arrived and that he was to be its champion instead of its opponent. To help the movement gain a foothold, Murray traveled around the country preaching about this new thing that was happening. Everywhere he went, revival broke out.

As with any true revival of the Holy Spirit, this was a revival of prayer. People who had seldom been to church in their lives would come to prayer meetings daily and sometimes even more than once a day. And where it had been difficult to find people to join the ministry prior to this time, as the revival spread, young men began stepping forward to offer themselves for the preaching of the Word.

Looking back on these exciting times as well as the lessons of humility God had taught him, Murray later wrote, "If only we did not so often hinder Him with our much trying to serve. How surely and mightily He would accomplish His own work of renewing souls into the likeness of Jesus Christ."

In 1864, Andrew was made pastor of a large church in Cape Town, where he stayed until 1871. In 1871, probably because of failing health, he transferred to a smaller church in Wellington, forty-five miles away. In many ways this turned out to be very fortunate for both his contemporaries and the generations that have followed; for during his time in Wellington, he began to write down his thoughts about his spiritual experiences and to share his accumulated knowledge on the Holy Spirit working in people's lives.

His books about Church renewal, revival, and the deeper spiritual life flowed from his pen like a river—eventually including over 250 titles, some of which were translated into multiple languages. Many of these reflect his continued theme of the quest for a deeper life in Christ: *The True Vine, Abide in Christ, Absolute Surrender, The Prayer Life, The Lord's Table, How to Raise Your Children for Christ, With Christ in the School of Prayer,* and *Be Perfect.*

In 1879 Murray lost his voice and had to give up preaching. He tried everything he could think of to regain it, but nothing worked. He and Emma moved back to London in 1882, hoping that rest and a change of climate would cure him. His plan was to consult the best physicians in England. But when he returned, he met a minister named Stockmaier who had written several books on healing through prayer. Over the next few weeks, they had several meetings that resulted in Murray checking into a residential healing center in London, and making arrangements to spend time in Bible study and prayer during his stay. Not long after taking up residence there, he attended a healing service during which he was anointed with oil while people prayed over him. His throat was instantly and permanently healed. He and Emma returned to Africa shortly thereafter.

In 1884 he wrote a book called *Divine Healing*, which recounted his experiences and promoted spiritual healing. It was an instant success. Unfortunately, it turned out to be too much of a good thing for the Dutch Reformed Church. All over South Africa people who had read the book went to their pastors to be healed, only to find that most of the clergy did not believe in healing prayer or have faith strong enough to accomplish it. This problem became so pervasive that the church forced Murray to withdraw the book from publication. It has rarely been published since.

Toward the end of his career, Murray traveled around the world proclaiming the Gospel of Christ and promoting the deeper spiritual life. For a while he joined D. L. Moody and Ira Sankey during their evangelistic tour in England. Then afterward he returned with them to the United States where he preached and taught at Moody's school in Northfield, Massachusetts.

After suffering a stroke, Emma died in January of 1905. A year later Andrew retired from the pastorate, but continued on for several more years with his writing, traveling, and preaching. In his later years, however, he rarely ventured from Wellington, where he passed away on January 18, 1917 at the age of 88.

Although his voice was stilled, his ministry lives on in books and treatises that were designed to feed the spiritual hunger of all those who seek a relationship with Jesus Christ. In Murray's work, Christ stands and beckons to us, inviting us to a deeper life with our Maker. You are about to read one of his best and most famous works. There is so much wisdom and richness of thought in *Absolute Surrender* that it bears reading multiple times; and it is almost a certainty that your understanding of your spiritual journey will be enhanced.

Andrew Murray
1828-1917

The house in which Andrew Murray was born,
known as "the old Parsonage," which later became
the home of his son Charles

Andrew Murray's father and mother

Andrew Murray as a young student

Marischal College, Aberdeen

Andrew Murray as
a young minister

John Murray,
Andrew's brother,
as a young minister

The Murray family in 1873.
Andrew is in the back row with his arm
affectionately around his wife Emma

1866 painting of Adderly Street, Cape Town, with the
Dutch Reformed Church in the background

Worcester, South Africa, about 1877.
The town of Andrew Murray's pastorate where great
revival broke out (1860–1864).

Andrew Murray, 43 years old, accepts the call
to the parsonage in the small South African
town of Wellington

Andrew Murray (center) and his family about 1880

Andrew Murray's dwelling, "Clairvaux" (on right)
with the Training Institute for Missionaries (to the left)

Professor Murray, age 70

The beach house at Kalk Bay, which Mr. Murray
affectionately called "Patmos"

On the rocks at "Patmos,"
Mr. Murray's favorite place of retreat

Andrew and Emma Murray

Andrew Murray unveiling the monument to his two
colleagues, Professors J. Murray and N. Hofmeyr, 1915

Andrew Murray shortly before his death
on January 18, 1917

CHAPTER 1

Absolute Surrender

And Ben-hadad the king of Syria gathered all his host together: and there were thirty and two kings with him, and horses, and chariots: and he went up and besieged Samaria, and warred against it. And he sent messengers to Ahab king of Israel into the city, and said unto him, Thus saith Ben-hadad, Thy silver and thy gold is mine; thy wives also and thy children, even the goodliest, are mine.
And the king of Israel answered and said, My lord, O king, according to thy saying, I am thine and all that I have. (1 Kings 20: 1-4)

What Ben Hadad asked was absolute surrender, and what Ahab gave was what was asked of him—absolute surrender. I want to use these words, "My lord, O king, according to thy saying, I am thine, and all that I have," as the words of absolute surrender with which every child of God ought to yield himself to his Father. We have heard it before, but we need to hear it very definitely—the condition of God's blessing is absolute surrender of all into His hands. Praise God! If our hearts are willing for that, there is no end to what God will do for us, and to the blessing He will bestow.

Absolute surrender—let me tell you where I got those words. I used them myself often, and you have heard them numberless times. But in Scotland, I once was in a company where we were talking about the condition of Christ's Church, and what the great need of the Church and believers is. There was in our company a godly worker who has much to do with training workers, and I asked him what he would say was the great need of the Church and the message that ought to be preached. He answered very quietly, simply, and determinedly, "Absolute surrender to God is the one thing."

The words struck me as never before. And that man began to tell how, in the workers with whom he had to deal, he finds that if they are sound on that point, even though they be backward, they are willing to be taught and helped, and they always improve; whereas others who are not sound there very often go back and leave the work. The condition for obtaining God's full blessing is absolute surrender to Him.

And now, I desire by God's grace to give to you this message—that your God in Heaven answers the prayers which you have offered for blessing on yourselves and for blessing on those around you by this one demand: Are you willing to surrender yourselves absolutely into His hands? What is our answer to be? God knows there are hundreds of hearts who have said it, and there are hundreds more who long to say it, but hardly dare to do so. And there are hearts who have said it, but who have yet miserably failed, and who feel themselves condemned because they did not find the secret of the power to live that life. May God have a word for all!

Let me say, first of all, that God claims it from us.

God Expects Your Surrender

Yes, it has its foundation in the very nature of God. God cannot do otherwise. Who is God? He is the Fountain of life, the only Source of existence and power and goodness, and throughout the universe there is nothing good but what God works. God has created the sun, the moon, the stars, the flowers, the trees, and the grass; and are they not all absolutely surrendered to God? Do they not allow God to work in them just what He pleases? When God clothes the lily with its beauty, is it not yielded up, surrendered, and given over to God as He works its beauty in it? And God's redeemed children—oh, can you think that God can work His work if there is only half or a part of them surrendered? God cannot do it. God is life, and love, and blessing, and power, and infinite beauty, and God delights to communicate himself to every child who is prepared to receive Him. But, ah! this one lack of absolute surrender is just the thing that hinders God. And now He comes, and as God, He claims it.

You know in daily life what absolute surrender is. You know that everything has to be given up to its special, definite object and service. I have a pen in my pocket. That pen is absolutely surrendered to the one work of writing, and that pen must be absolutely surrendered to my hand if I am to write properly with it. If another holds it partly, I cannot write properly. This coat is absolutely given up to me to cover my body. This building is entirely given up to religious services. And now, do you expect that in your immortal being, in the divine nature that you have received by regeneration, God can work His work, every day and every hour, unless you are entirely given up to Him? God cannot. The Temple of Solomon was absolutely surrendered to God when it was dedicated to Him. And every one of us is a temple of God, in which God will dwell and work mightily on one condition—absolute surrender to Him. God claims it; God is worthy of it; and without it, God cannot work His blessed work in us.

God not only claims it, but God will work it himself.

God Accomplishes Your Surrender

I am sure there is a heart that says, "Ah, but that absolute surrender implies so much!" Someone says, "Oh, I have passed through so much trial and suffering, and there is so much of the self-life still remaining, and I dare not face the entire giving of it up, because I know it will cause so much trouble and agony."

Alas! alas! that God's children have such thoughts of Him, such cruel thoughts. Oh, I come to you with a message, fearful and anxious one. God does not ask you to give the perfect surrender in your strength, or by the power of your will; God is willing to work it in you. Do we not read, "It is God that worketh in us, both to will and to do of his good pleasure"? And that is what we should seek for—to go on our faces before God, until our hearts learn to believe that the everlasting God himself will come in to turn out what is wrong, to conquer what is evil, and to work what is well-pleasing in His blessed sight. God himself will work it in you.

Look at the men in the Old Testament, men like Abraham. Do you think it was by accident that God found that man, the father of the faithful and the Friend of God, and that it was Abraham himself, apart from God, who had such faith and such obedience and such devotion? You

26

know it is not so. God raised him up and prepared him as an instrument for His glory.

Did not God say to Pharaoh, "For this cause have I raised thee up, for to show in thee my power"?

And if God said that of him, will not God say it far more of every child of His?

Oh, I want to encourage you, and I want you to cast away every fear. Come with that feeble desire; and if there is the fear, which says, "Oh, my desire is not strong enough, I am not willing for everything that may come, I do not feel bold enough to say I can conquer everything"—I pray you, learn to know and trust your God now. Say, "My God, I am willing that Thou shouldst make me willing." If there is anything holding you back, or any sacrifice you are afraid of making, come to God now, and prove how gracious your God is, and be not afraid that He will command from you what He will not bestow.

God comes and offers to work this absolute surrender in you. All these searchings, hungerings, and longings that are in your heart, I tell you they are the drawings of the divine magnet, Christ Jesus. He lived a life of absolute surrender, He has possession of you; He is living in your heart by His Holy Spirit. You have hindered, and hindered Him terribly, but He desires to help you to get hold of Him entirely. And He comes and draws you now by His message and words. Will you not come and trust God to work in you that absolute surrender to himself? Yes, blessed be God, He can do it, and He will do it.

God not only claims it and works it, but God accepts it when we bring it to Him.

God Accepts Your Surrender

God works it in the secret of our heart; God urges us by the hidden power of His Holy Spirit to come and speak it out, and we have to bring and to yield to Him that absolute surrender. But remember, when you come and bring God that absolute surrender, it may, as far as your feelings (your consciousness) go, be a thing of great imperfection, and you may doubt and hesitate and say:

"Is it absolute?"

But, oh, remember there was once a man to whom Christ had said, "If thou canst believe, all things are possible to him that believeth."

And his heart was afraid, and he cried out, "Lord, I believe; help thou mine unbelief."

That was a faith that triumphed over the devil, and the evil spirit was cast out. And if you come and say, "Lord, I yield myself in absolute surrender to my God," even though it is with a trembling heart and with this consciousness, "I do not feel the power; I do not feel the determination; I do not feel the assurance," it will succeed. Be not afraid, but come just as you are, and even in the midst of your trembling the power of the Holy Ghost will work.

Have you never yet learned the lesson that the Holy Ghost works with mighty power, while on the human side everything appears feeble? Look at the Lord Jesus Christ in Gethsemane. We read that He, "through the eternal Spirit," offered himself a sacrifice unto God. The Almighty Spirit of God was enabling Him to do it. Yet, what agony, fear, and exceeding sorrow came over Him, and how He prayed!

Externally, you can see no sign of the mighty power of the Spirit, but the Spirit of God was there. Even so, while you are feeble, fighting, and trembling, in faith in the hidden work of God's Spirit do not fear, but yield yourself.

When you do yield yourself in absolute surrender, let it be in the faith that God does now accept of it. That is the great point, and that is what we so often miss—that believers should be thus occupied with God in this matter of surrender. I pray you, be occupied with God. We want to get help, every one of us, so that in our daily life God shall be clearer to us, God shall have the right place, and be "all in all." And if we are to have that through life, let us begin now and look away from ourselves, and look up to God. Let each believe—while I, a poor worm on Earth and a trembling child of God, full of failure and sin and fear, bow here; and no one knows what passes through my heart, and while I in simplicity say, "O God, I accept Thy terms. I have pleaded for blessing on others and myself. I have accepted Thy terms of absolute surrender." While your heart says that in deep silence, remember that God is present and takes note of it, and writes it down in His book. God is present, and at that very moment, takes possession of you. You may not feel it, you may not realize it, but God takes possession if you will trust Him.

God not only claims it, and works it, and accepts it when I bring it, but also maintains it.

God Maintains Your Surrender

That is the great difficulty with many. People say, "I have often been stirred at a meeting, or at a convention, and I have consecrated myself to God, but it has passed away. I know it may last for a week or for a month, but away it fades, and after a time it is all gone."

But listen! It is because you do not believe what I am now going to tell you and remind you of. When God has begun the work of absolute surrender in you, and when God has accepted your surrender, then God holds himself bound to care for it and to keep it. Will you believe that?

In this matter of surrender, there are two: God and I—I, a worm, and God, the everlasting and omnipotent Jehovah. Worm, will you be afraid to trust yourself to this mighty God now? God is willing. Do you not believe that He can keep you continually, day by day, and moment by moment?

Moment by moment, I am kept in His love;
Moment by moment, I have life from above.

If God allows the sun to shine upon you moment by moment, without intermission, will not He let His life shine upon you every moment? And why have you not experienced it? Because you have not trusted God for it, and you do not surrender yourself absolutely to Him in that trust.

A life of absolute surrender has its difficulties. I do not deny that. Yes, it has something far more than difficulties: it is a life that with men is absolutely impossible. But by the grace of God, by the power of God, by the power of the Holy Spirit dwelling in us, it is a life to which we are destined, and a life that is possible for us, praise God! Let us believe that God will maintain it.

Some of you have read the words of that aged saint who, on his ninetieth birthday, told of all God's goodness to him—I mean George Muller. What did he say he believed to be the secret of his happiness, and of all the blessing, which God had given him? He said he believed there were two reasons. The one was that he had been enabled by grace to maintain a good conscience before God day by day; the other was that he was a lover of God's Word. Ah, yes, a good conscience is complete obedience to God day by day, and fellowship with God every day in His Word, and prayer—that is a life of absolute surrender.

Such a life has two sides—on the one side, absolute surrender to work what God wants you to do; on the other side, to let God work what He wants to do.

First, to do what God wants you to do.

Give up yourselves absolutely to the will of God. You know something of that will—not enough, far from all. But say absolutely to the Lord God, "By Thy grace I desire to do Thy will in everything, every moment of every day." Say, "Lord God, not a word upon my tongue but for Thy glory, not a movement of my temper but for Thy glory, not an affection of love or hate in my heart but for Thy glory, and according to Thy blessed will."

Someone says, "Do you think that possible?"

I ask, "What has God promised you, and what can God do to fill a vessel absolutely surrendered to Him?" Oh, God wants to bless you in a way beyond what you expect. From the beginning, ear hath not heard, neither hath the eye seen, what God hath prepared for them that wait for Him. God has prepared unheard of things, blessings much more

31

wonderful than you can imagine, more mighty than you can conceive. They are divine blessings. Oh, say now:

"I give myself absolutely to God, to His will, to do only what God wants."

God will enable you to carry out the surrender.

And, on the other side, come and say, "I give myself absolutely to God, to let Him work in me to will and to do of His good pleasure, as He has promised to do."

Yes, the living God wants to work in His children in a way that we cannot understand, but that God's Word has revealed, and He wants to work in us every moment of the day. God is willing to maintain our life. Only let our absolute surrender be one of simple, childlike, and unbounded trust.

God Blesses When You Surrender

This absolute surrender to God will wonderfully bless.

What Ahab said to his enemy, King Ben-hadad—"My lord, O king, according to thy word I am thine, and all that I have"—shall we not say the same to our God and loving Father? If we do say it, God's blessing will come upon us. God wants us to be separate from the world; we are called to come out from the world that hates God. Come out for God, and say, "Lord, anything for thee." If you say that with prayer, and speak that into God's ear, He will accept it, and He will teach you what it means.

I say again, God will bless you. You have been praying for blessing. But do remember, there must be absolute surrender. At every tea table, you see it. Why is tea poured into a cup? Because it is empty, and given up for the tea. But put ink, or vinegar, or wine into it, and will they pour tea into the vessel? And can God fill you, can God bless you if you are not absolutely surrendered to Him? He cannot. Let us believe God has wonderful blessings for us, if we will but stand up for Him, and say, be it with a trembling will, yet with a believing heart:

"O God, I accept Thy demands. I am thine and all that I have. Absolute surrender is what my soul yields to Thee by divine grace."

You may not have such strong and clear feelings of deliverance as you would desire to have, but humble yourselves in His sight, and acknowledge that you have grieved the Holy Spirit by your self-will, self-confidence, and self-effort. Bow humbly before Him in the confession of that, and ask Him to break your heart and bring you into the dust before Him. Then, as you bow before Him, just accept God's teaching that in your flesh "there dwelleth no good thing," and that nothing will help you except another life, which must come in. You must deny self once for all. Denying self must every moment be the power of your life, and then Christ will come in and take possession of you.

When was Peter delivered? When was the change accomplished? The change began with Peter weeping, and the Holy Ghost came down and filled his heart.

God the Father loves to give us the power of the Spirit. We have the Spirit of God dwelling within us. We come to God confessing that, praising God for it, and yet confessing

33

how we have grieved the Spirit. And then we bow our knees to the Father to ask that He would strengthen us with all might by the Spirit in the inner man, and that He would fill us with His mighty power. And as the Spirit reveals Christ to us, Christ comes to live in our hearts forever, and the self-life is cast out.

Let us bow before God in humility, and in that humility, confess before Him the state of the whole Church. No words can tell the sad state of the Church of Christ on Earth. I wish I had words to speak what I sometimes feel about it. Just think of the Christians around you. I do not speak of nominal Christians or of professing Christians, but I speak of hundreds and thousands of honest, earnest Christians who are not living a life in the power of God or to His glory. So little power, so little devotion or consecration to God, so little perception of the truth that a Christian is a man utterly surrendered to God's will! Oh, we want to confess the sins of God's people around us, and to humble ourselves. We are members of that sickly body, and the sickliness of the body will hinder us, and break us down, unless we come to God, and in confession separate ourselves from partnership with worldliness, with coldness toward each other, unless we give up ourselves to be entirely and wholly for God.

How much Christian work is being done in the spirit of the flesh and in the power of self! How much work, day by day, in which human energy—our will and our thoughts about the work—is continually manifested, and in which there is but little of waiting upon God, and upon the power of the Holy Ghost! Let us make confession. But as we confess the state of the Church and the feebleness and sinfulness of work for God among us, let us come back to ourselves. Who is there who truly longs to be delivered

34

from the power of the self-life, who truly acknowledges that it is the power of self and the flesh, and who is willing to cast all at the feet of Christ? That is where deliverance is found.

I heard of one who had been an earnest Christian, and who spoke about the "cruel" thought of separation and death. But you do not think that, do you? What are we to think of separation and death? This: Death was the path to glory for Christ. For the joy set before Him He endured the cross. The cross was the birthplace of His everlasting glory. Do you love Christ? Do you long to be in Christ? Let death be to you the most desirable thing on Earth—death to self, and fellowship with Christ. Separation—do you think it is a hard thing to be called to be entirely free from the world, and by that separation to be united to God and His love, by separation to become prepared for living and walking with God every day? Surely, one ought to say, "Anything to bring me to separation, to death, for a life of full fellowship with God and Christ."

Come and cast this self-life and flesh-life at the feet of Jesus. Then trust Him. Do not worry yourselves with trying to understand all about it, but come in the living faith that Christ will come into you with the power of His death and the power of His life; and then the Holy Spirit will bring the whole Christ—Christ crucified and risen and living in glory—into your heart.

CHAPTER 2

The Fruit of the Spirit Is Love

*F*want to look at the fact of a life filled with the Holy Spirit more from the practical side, and to show how this life will show itself in our daily walk and conduct.

Under the Old Testament, you know the Holy Spirit often came upon men as a divine Spirit of revelation to reveal the mysteries of God, or for power to do the work of God. But He did not then dwell in them. Now, many just want the Old Testament gift of power for work, but know very little of the New Testament gift of the indwelling Spirit, animating and renewing the whole life. When God gives the Holy Spirit, His great object is the formation of a holy character. It is a gift of a holy mind and spiritual disposition, and what we need above everything else, is to say:

> *"I must have the Holy Spirit sanctifying my whole inner life if I am really to live for God's glory."*

You might say that when Christ promised the Spirit to the disciples, He did so that they might have power to be witnesses. True, but then they received the Holy Ghost in such heavenly power and reality that He took possession of their whole being at once and so fitted them as holy men for doing the work with power as they had to do it. Christ spoke of power to the disciples, but it was the Spirit filling their whole being that worked the power.

I wish now to dwell upon the passage found in Galatians 5:22:

"The fruit of the Spirit is love."

We read that "Love is the fulfilling of the law," and my desire is to speak on love as a fruit of the Spirit with a twofold object. One is that this word may be a searchlight in our hearts, and give us a test by which to try all our thoughts about the Holy Spirit and all our experience of the holy life. Let us try ourselves by this word. Has this been our daily habit, to seek the being filled with the Holy Spirit as the Spirit of love? "The fruit of the Spirit is love." Has it been our experience that the more we have of the Holy Spirit, the more loving we become? In claiming the Holy Spirit, we should make this the first object of our expectation. The Holy Spirit comes as a Spirit of love.

Oh, if this were true in the Church of Christ, how different her state would be! May God help us to get hold of this simple, heavenly truth that the fruit of the Spirit is a love which appears in the life, and that just as the Holy Spirit gets real possession of the life, the heart will be filled with real, divine, universal love.

One of the great reasons that God cannot bless His Church is the lack of love. When the body is divided, there cannot be strength. In the time of their great religious wars, when Holland stood out so nobly against Spain, one of their mottoes was, "Unity gives strength." It is only when God's people stand as one body, one before God in the fellowship of love, one toward another in deep affection, one before the world in a love that the world can see—it is only then that they will have power to secure the blessing which they ask of God. Remember that if a vessel that ought to be one whole is cracked into many pieces, it cannot be filled. You can take a potsherd, one part of a vessel, and dip out a little water into that, but if you want the vessel full, the vessel must be whole. That is literally true of Christ's Church, and if there is one thing we must pray for still, it is this: Lord, melt us together into one by the power of the Holy Spirit; let the Holy Spirit, who at Pentecost made them all of one heart and one soul, do His blessed work among us. Praise God, we can love each other in a divine love, for "the fruit of the Spirit is love." Give yourselves up to love, and the Holy Spirit will come. Receive the Spirit, and He will teach you to love more.

God Is Love

Now, why is it that the fruit of the Spirit is love? Because God is love. And what does that mean?

It is the very nature and being of God to delight in communicating himself. God has no selfishness; God keeps nothing to himself. God's nature is to be always giving. In the sun and the moon and the stars, in every flower, in every bird in the air, and in every fish in the sea yo usee it. God communicates life to His creatures. And the angels around His throne, the seraphim and cherubim who are flames of fire, whence have they their glory? It is because God is love, and He imparts to them of His brightness and His blessedness. And we, His redeemed children—God delights to pour His love into us. And why? Because, as I said, God keeps nothing for himself. From eternity, God had His only begotten Son. The Father gave Him all things, and nothing that God had was kept back. "God is love."

One of the old church fathers said that we cannot understand the Trinity better than as a revelation of divine love—the Father, the loving One, the Fountain of love; the Son, the beloved One, the Reservoir of love in whom the love was poured out; and the Spirit, the living love that united both and then overflowed into this world. The Spirit of Pentecost, the Spirit of the Father, and the Spirit of the Son is love. And when the Holy Spirit comes to us and to other men, will He be less a Spirit of love than He is in God? It cannot be; He cannot change His nature. The Spirit of God is love, and "the fruit of the Spirit is love."

Mankind Needs Love

Why is that so? That was the one great need of mankind; that was the thing which Christ's redemption came to accomplish: to restore love to this world.

When man sinned, why was it that he sinned? Selfishness triumphed—he sought self instead of God. And just look! Adam at once begins to accuse the woman of having led him astray. Love to God had gone, love to man was lost. Look again: of the first two children of Adam, the one becomes a murderer of his brother.

Does not that teach us that sin had robbed the world of love? Ah! What a proof of love having been lost! There may have been beautiful examples of love even among the heathen, but only as a little remnant of what was lost. One of the worst things sin did for man was to make him selfish, for selfishness cannot love.

The Lord Jesus Christ came down from Heaven as the Son of God's love. "God so loved the world that He gave His only begotten Son." God's Son came to show what love is, and He lived a life of love here upon Earth in fellowship with His disciples, in compassion over the poor and miserable, in love even to His enemies, and He died the death of love. And when He went to Heaven, whom did He send down? The Spirit of love, to come and banish selfishness and envy and pride, and bring the love of God into the hearts of men. "The fruit of the Spirit is love."

And what was the preparation for the promise of the Holy Spirit? You know that promise as found in the fourteenth chapter of John's gospel. But remember what precedes it in the thirteenth chapter. Before Christ promised the Holy Spirit, He gave a new commandment, and about that new commandment, He said wonderful things. One thing was, "Even as I have loved you, so love ye one another." To them, His dying love was to be the only law of their conduct and interaction with each other. What a message to those fishermen, to those men full of pride and selfishness! "Learn to love each other," said Christ, "as I have loved you." And by the grace of God, they did it. When Pentecost came, they were of one heart and one soul. Christ did it for them.

And now He calls us to dwell and to walk in love. He demands that though a man hates you, still you love him. True love cannot be conquered by anything in Heaven or upon the Earth. The more hatred there is, the more love triumphs through it all and shows its true nature. This is the love that Christ commanded His disciples to exercise.

What more did He say? "By this shall all men know that ye are my disciples, if ye have love one to another."

You all know what it is to wear a badge. And Christ said to His disciples in effect, "I give you a badge, and that badge is love. That is to be your mark. It is the only thing in Heaven or on Earth by which men can know me."

Do we not begin to fear that love has fled from the Earth? That if we were to ask the world, "Have you seen us wear the badge of love?" the world would say, "No, what we have heard of the Church of Christ is that there is not a place where there is no quarreling and separation." Let us ask God with one heart that we may wear the badge of Jesus' love. God is able to give it.

Love Conquers Selfishness

"The fruit of the Spirit is love." Why? Because nothing but love can expel and conquer our selfishness.

Self is the great curse, whether in its relation to God, or to our fellow men in general, or to fellow-Christians, thinking of ourselves and seeking our own. Self is our greatest curse. But, praise God, Christ came to redeem us from self. We sometimes talk about deliverance from the self-life—and thank God for every word that can be said about it to help us—but I am afraid some people think deliverance from the self-life means that now they are going to have no more trouble in serving God. They forget that deliverance from the self-life means to be a vessel overflowing with love for everybody all day.

And there you have the reason why many people pray for the power of the Holy Ghost, and they get something, but, oh, so little! because they prayed for power for work and power for blessing, but they have not prayed for power for full deliverance from self. That means not only the righteous self in interaction with God, but also the unloving self in interaction with men. And there is deliverance. "The fruit of the Spirit is love." I bring you the glorious promise of Christ that He is able to fill our hearts with love.

A great many of us try hard at times to love. We try to force ourselves to love, and I do not say that is wrong; it is better than nothing. But the end of it is always very sad. "I fail continually," such as one must confess. And what is the reason? The reason is simply this: Because they have never learned to believe and accept the truth that the Holy Spirit can pour God's love into their hearts. That blessed text; often it has been limited! —"The love of God is shed abroad in our hearts." It has often been understood in this sense: It means the love of God to me. Oh, what a limitation! That is only the beginning. The love of God is always the love of God in its entirety, in its fullness as an indwelling power, a love of God to me that leaps back to Him in love, and overflows to my fellow men in love—God's love to me, and my love to God, and my love to my fellow men. The three are one; you cannot separate them.

Do believe that the love of God can be shed abroad in your heart and mine so that we can love all the day.

"Ah!" you say, "how little I have understood that!"

Why is a lamb always gentle? Because that is its nature. Does it cost the lamb any trouble to be gentle? No. Why not? It is so beautiful and gentle. Does a lamb have to study to be gentle? No. Why does it come so easy? It is its nature. And a wolf—why does it cost a wolf no trouble to be cruel, and to put its fangs into the poor lamb or sheep?

Because that is its nature. It does not have to summon up its courage; the wolf-nature is there.

And how can I learn to love? Never until the Spirit of God fills my heart with God's love, and I begin to long for God's love in a very different sense from which I have sought it so selfishly, as a comfort and a joy and a happiness and a pleasure to myself; never until I begin to learn that "God is love," and to claim it, and receive it as an indwelling power for self-sacrifice; never until I begin to see that my glory, my blessedness, is to be like God and like Christ, in giving up everything in myself for my fellow-men. May God teach us that! Oh, the divine blessedness of the love with which the Holy Spirit can fill our hearts! "The fruit of the Spirit is love."

Love Is God's Gift

Once again, I ask, "Why must this be so?" And my answer is, "Without this, we cannot live the daily life of love."

How often, when we speak about the consecrated life, we have to speak about temper, and some people have sometimes said:

"You make too much of temper."

I do not think we can make too much of it. Think for a moment of a clock and of what its hands mean. The hands tell me what is within the clock, and if I see that the hands stand still, or that the hands point wrong, or that the clock is slow or fast, I say that something inside the clock is not working properly. And temper is just like the

44

revelation that the clock gives of what is within. Temper is a proof whether the love of Christ is filling the heart or not. How many there are who find it easier in church, or in prayer-meeting, or in work for the Lord—diligent, earnest work—to be holy and happy than in the daily life with wife and children and servant; easier to be holy and happy outside the home than in it! Where is the love of God? In Christ. God has prepared for us a wonderful redemption in Christ, and He longs to make something supernatural of us. Have we learned to long for it, ask for it, and expect it in its fullness?

Then there is the tongue! We sometimes speak of the tongue when we talk of the better life and the restful life, but just think what liberty many Christians give to their tongues. They say:

"I have a right to think what I like."

When they speak about each other, when they speak about their neighbors, when they speak about other Christians, how often there are sharp remarks! God, keep me from saying anything that would be unloving; God, shut my mouth if I am not to speak in tender love. But what I am saying is a fact. How often there are found among Christians who are banded together in work, sharp criticism, sharp judgment, hasty opinion, unloving words, secret contempt of each other, and secret condemnation of each other! Oh, just as a mother's love covers her children and delights in them and has the most tender compassion with their foibles or failures, so there ought to be in the heart of every believer a motherly love toward every brother and sister in Christ. Have you aimed at that? Have you sought it? Have you ever pleaded for it? Jesus Christ said, "As I have loved you ... love one another." And He did not put that among the other commandments, but He said in effect:

"That is a new commandment, the one commandment: Love one another as I have loved you."

It is in our daily life and conduct that the fruit of the Spirit is love. From that, there come all the graces and virtues in which love is manifested: joy, peace, longsuffering, gentleness, goodness; no sharpness or hardness in your tone, no unkindness or selfishness; meekness before God and man. You see that all these are the gentler virtues. I have often thought as I read those words in Colossians, "Put on therefore as the elect of God, holy and beloved, bowels of mercies, kindness, humbleness of mind, meekness, longsuffering," that if we had written them, we should have put in the foreground the manly virtues, such as zeal, courage, and diligence. But we need to see how the gentler, the womanliest virtues are specially connected with dependence upon the Holy Spirit. These are indeed heavenly graces. They never were found in the heathen world. Christ was needed to come from Heaven to teach us. Your blessedness is longsuffering, meekness, kindness; your glory is humility before God. The fruit of the Spirit that He brought from Heaven out of the heart of the crucified Christ, and that He gives in our heart, is first and foremost—love.

You know what John says. "No man hath seen God at any time. If we love one another, God dwelleth in us." That is, I cannot see God, but as compensation, I can see my brother, and if I love him, God dwells in me. Is that really true? That I cannot see God, but I must love my brother, and God will dwell in me? Loving my brother is

46

the way to real fellowship with God. You know what John further says in that most solemn test, "If a man say, I love God, and hateth his brother, he is a liar; for he that loveth not his brother whom he hath seen, how can he love God whom he hath not seen?" (1 John 4:20). There is a brother, a most unlovable man. He worries you every time you meet him. He is of the very opposite disposition to yours. You are a careful businessman, and you have to do with him in your business. He is most untidy, unbusinesslike. You say, "I cannot love him."

Oh, friend, you have not learned the lesson that Christ wanted to teach above everything. Let a man be what he will, you are to love him. Love is to be the fruit of the Spirit all the day and every day. Yes, listen! If a man does not love his brother whom he has seen—if you do not love that unlovable man whom you have seen, how can you love God whom you have not seen? You can deceive yourself with beautiful thoughts about loving God. You must prove your love to God by your love to your brother; that is the one standard by which God will judge your love to Him. If the love of God is in your heart, you will love your brother. The fruit of the Spirit is love.

And what is the reason that God's Holy Spirit cannot come in power? Is it not possible?

You remember the comparison I used in speaking of the vessel. I can dip a little water into a potsherd, a bit of a vessel, but if a vessel is to be full, it must be unbroken. And the children of God, wherever they come together, to whatever church or mission or society they belong, must love each other intensely, or the Spirit of God cannot do His work. We talk about grieving the Spirit of God by worldliness and ritualism and formality and error and indifference, but, I tell you, the one thing above everything that grieves God's Spirit is this want of love. Let every heart search itself, and ask that God may search it.

Our Love Shows God's Power

Why are we taught, "The fruit of the Spirit is love"? Because the Spirit of God has come to make our daily life an exhibition of divine power and a revelation of what God can do for His children.

In the second and the fourth chapters of Acts, we read that the disciples were of one heart and of one soul. During the three years they had walked with Christ they never had been in that spirit. All Christ's teaching could not make them of one heart and one soul. But the Holy Spirit came from Heaven and shed the love of God in their hearts, and they were of one heart and one soul. The same Holy Spirit that brought the love of Heaven into their hearts must fill us too. Nothing less will do. Even as Christ did, one might preach love for three years with the tongue of an angel, but that would not teach any man to love unless the power of the Holy Spirit should come upon him to bring the love of Heaven into his heart.

Think of the church at large. What divisions! Think of the different bodies. Take the question of holiness, the question of the cleansing blood, and the question of the baptism of the Spirit—what differences are caused among dear believers by such questions! That there are differences of opinion does not trouble me. We do not all have the same constitution and temperament and mind. But how often hate, bitterness, contempt, separation, and unlovingness are caused by the holiest truths of God's Word! Our doctrines, our creeds, have been more important than love. We often think we are valiant for the truth and we forget God's command to speak the truth in love. And it was so in the time of the Reformation between the Lutheran and Calvinistic churches. What bitterness there was then in regard to the Holy Supper, which was meant to be the bond of union among all believers! And so, down the ages, the very dearest truths of God have become mountains that have separated us.

If we want to pray in power, if we want to expect the Holy Spirit to come down in power, and if we want, indeed, that God shall pour out His Spirit, we must enter into a covenant with God that we love one another with a heavenly love.

Are you ready for that? Only that love is true love that is large enough to take in all God's children, the most unloving and unlovable, and unworthy, and unbearable, and trying. If my vow—absolute surrender to God—was true, then it must mean absolute surrender to the divine love to fill me; to be a servant of love to love every child of God around me. "The fruit of the Spirit is love."

Oh, God did something wonderful when He gave Christ, at His right hand, the Holy Spirit to come down out of the heart of the Father and His everlasting love. And how we have degraded the Holy Spirit into a mere power by which we have to do our work! God forgive us! Oh, that the Holy Spirit might be held in honor as a power to fill us with the very life and nature of God and of Christ!

Christian Work Requires Love

"The fruit of the Spirit is love." I ask once again, "Why is it so?" And the answer comes, "That is the only power in which Christians really can do their work."

Yes, that is what we need. We want not only love that is to bind us to each other, but we want a divine love in our work for the lost around us. Oh, do we not often undertake a great deal of work, just as men undertake works of philanthropy from a natural spirit of compassion for our fellow men? Do we not often undertake Christian work because our minister or friend calls us to it? And do we not often perform Christian work with certain zeal, but without having had a baptism of love?

People often ask, "What is the baptism of fire?"

I have answered more than once: I know no fire like the fire of God, the fire of everlasting love that consumed the sacrifice on Calvary. The baptism of love is what the Church needs, and to get that, we must begin at once to get down upon our faces before God in confession and plead:

"Lord, let love from Heaven flow down into my heart. I am giving up my life to pray and live as one who has given himself up for the everlasting love to dwell in and fill him."

Ah, yes, if the love of God were in our hearts, what a difference it would make! There are hundreds of believers who say, "I work for Christ, and I feel I could work much harder, but I have not the gift. I do not know how or where to begin. I do not know what I can do."

Brother, sister, ask God to baptize you with the Spirit of love, and love will find its way. Love is a fire that will burn through every difficulty. You may be a shy, hesitating man, who cannot speak well, but love can burn through everything. God, fill us with love! We need it for our work.

You have read many touching stories of love expressed, and you have said, "How beautiful!" I heard one of these stories not long ago. A lady had been asked to speak at a Rescue Home where there were a number of poor women. As she arrived there and got to the window with the matron, she saw a wretched person sitting outside and asked, "Who is that?"

The matron answered, "She has been into the house thirty or forty times, and she has always gone away again. Nothing can be done with her, she is so low and hard."

But the lady said, "She must come in."

The matron then said, "We have been waiting for you, and the company is assembled, and you have only an hour for the address."

The lady replied, "No, this is of more importance." And she went outside where the woman was sitting and asked, "My sister, what is the matter?"

"I am not your sister," was the reply.
Then the lady laid her hand on her, and said, "Yes, I am your sister, and I love you." She spoke like this until the heart of the poor woman was touched.

The conversation lasted some time while the company waited patiently. Ultimately, the lady brought the woman into the room. There was the poor wretched, degraded creature, full of shame. She would not sit on a chair, but sat down on a stool beside the speaker's seat, and she let her lean against her, with her arms around the poor woman's neck, while she spoke to the assembled people. And that love touched the woman's heart; she had found one who really loved her, and that love gave access to the love of Jesus.

Praise God! there is love upon Earth in the hearts of God's children, but, oh, that there were more!

O God, baptize our ministers with a tender love, and our missionaries, and our colporteurs [peddlers of religious books], and our Bible-readers, and our workers, and our young men's and young women's associations. Oh, that God would begin with us now, and baptize us with heavenly love!

Love Inspires Intercession

Once again: It is only love that can fit us for the work of intercession.

I have said that love must fit us for our work. Do you know what the hardest and the most important work is that has to be done for this sinful world? It is the work of intercession, the work of going to God and taking time to lay hold on Him.

A man may be an earnest Christian, an earnest minister, and a man who may do good, but alas! how often he has

52

to confess that he knows but little of what it is to tarry with God. May God give us the great gift of an intercessory spirit, a spirit of prayer and supplication! Let me ask you in the name of Jesus not to let a day pass without praying for all saints, and for all God's people.

I find there are Christians who think little of that. I find there are prayer unions where they pray for the members, and not for all believers. I pray you, take time to pray for the Church of Jesus Christ. It is right to pray for the heathen, as I have already said. God help us to pray more for them. It is right to pray for missionaries and for evangelistic work, and for the unconverted. But Paul did not tell people to pray for the heathen or the unconverted. Paul told them to pray for believers. Make this your first prayer every day, "Lord, bless thy saints everywhere."

The state of Christ's Church is indescribably low. Plead for God's people that He would visit them, plead for each other, and plead for all believers who are trying to work for God. Let love fill your heart. Ask Christ to pour it out afresh into you every day. Try to get it into you by the Holy Spirit of God: I am separated unto the Holy Spirit, and the fruit of the Spirit is love. God, help us to understand it.

May God grant that we learn day by day to wait more quietly upon Him. Do not wait upon God only for ourselves, or the power to do so will soon be lost. Give ourselves up to the ministry and the love of intercession, and pray more for God's people, for God's people round about us, for the Spirit of love in ourselves and in them, and for the work of God with whom we are connected. The answer will surely come, and our waiting upon God will be a source of untold blessing and power. "The fruit of the Spirit is love."

Have you a lack of love to confess before God? Then make confession and say before Him, "O Lord, my lack of heart, my lack of love—I confess it." And then, as you cast that lack at His feet, believe that the blood cleanses you, that Jesus comes in His mighty, cleansing, saving power to deliver you, and that He will give His Holy Spirit.

"The fruit of the Spirit is love."

CHAPTER 3

Separated Unto the Holy Ghost

*Now there were in the church that was at Antioch
certain prophets and teachers; as Barnabas,
and Simeon that was called Niger, and Lucius
of Cyrene, and Manaen ... and Saul. As they
ministered to the Lord, and fasted, the Holy Ghost
said, Separate me Barnabas and Saul for the work
whereunto I have called them. And when they had
fasted and prayed, and laid their hands on them,
they sent them away. So they, being sent forth by
the Holy Ghost, departed unto Seleucia.
(Acts 13:1-4)*

In the story of our text, we shall find some precious
thoughts to guide us as to what God would have
of us, and what God would do for us. The great
lesson of the verses quoted is this: The Holy Ghost is the
director of the work of God upon the earth. If we are to
work rightly for God, and if God is to bless our work, we
should stand in a right relation to the Holy Ghost, so that
every day we give Him the place of honor that belongs to
Him, and that in all our work and (what is more) in all
our private inner life, the Holy Ghost shall always have the
first place. Let me point out to you some of the precious
thoughts our passage suggests.

First of all, we see that God has His own plans with regard to His kingdom.

His church at Antioch had been established. God had certain plans and intentions with regard to Asia, and with regard to Europe. He had conceived them; they were His, and He made them known to His servants.

Our great Commander organizes every campaign, and His generals and officers do not always know the great plans. They often receive sealed orders, and they have to wait on Him for what He gives them as orders. God in Heaven has wishes, and a will, in regard to any work that ought to be done, and to the way in which it has to be done. Blessed is the man who gets into God's secrets and works under God.

Some years ago, at Wellington, South Africa, where I live, we opened a mission institute—a fine, large building. At our opening services, the principal said something I have never forgotten.

He remarked, "Last year we gathered here to lay the foundation-stone. What was there then to be seen? Nothing but rubbish, and stones, and bricks, and ruins of an old building that had been pulled down. There we laid the foundation stone, and very few knew what the building was that was to rise. No one knew it perfectly in every detail except one man, the architect."

In his mind it was all clear, and as the contractor and the mason and the carpenter came to their work, they took their orders from him, and the humblest laborer had to be obedient to orders, and the structure rose, and this beautiful building has been completed.

"And just so," he added. "This building that we open today is but laying the foundation of a work of which only God knows what is to become."

But God has His workers and His plans clearly mapped out, and our position is to wait, that God should communicate to us as much of His will as each time is needful.

We have simply to be faithful in obedience, carrying out His orders. God has a plan for His Church upon Earth. But alas! we too often make our plan, and we think that we know what ought to be done. We ask God first to bless our feeble efforts, instead of absolutely refusing to go unless God goes before us. God has planned for the work and the extension of His kingdom. The Holy Ghost has had that work given in charge to Him. "The work whereunto I have called them." May God, therefore, help us all to be afraid of touching "the ark of God," except as we are led by the Holy Ghost.

Then the second thought—God is willing and able to reveal to His servants what His will is.

Yes, blessed be God, communications still come down from Heaven! As we read here what the Holy Ghost said, so the Holy Ghost will still speak to His Church and His people. In these later days, He has often done it. He has come to individual men, and by His divine teaching He has led them out into fields of labor that others could not at first understand or approve, into ways and methods that did not recommend themselves to the majority. But in our time, the Holy Ghost does still teach His people. Thank God, in our foreign missionary societies and in our home missions, and in a thousand forms of work, the guiding of the Holy Ghost is known, but (we are all ready, I think, to confess) too little known. We have not learned enough to wait upon Him, and so we should make a solemn declaration before God: O God, we want to wait more for Thee to show us Thy will.

Do not ask God only for power. Many a Christian has his own plan of working, but God must send the power. The man works in his own will, and God must give the grace—the one reason why God often gives so little grace and so little success. But let us all take our place before God and say:

"What is done in the will of God, the strength of God will not be withheld from it; what is done in the will of God must have the mighty blessing of God."

And so let our first desire be to have the will of God revealed.

If you ask me, "Is it an easy thing to get these communications from Heaven, and to understand them?" I can give you the answer. It is easy to those who are in right fellowship with Heaven, and who understand the art of waiting upon God in prayer.

How often we ask: "How can a person know the will of God?" And people want, when they are in perplexity, to pray very earnestly that God should answer them at once. But God can only reveal His will to a heart that is humble, tender, and empty. God can only reveal His will in perplexities and special difficulties to a heart that has learned to obey and honor Him loyally in little things and in daily life.

That brings me to the third thought—Note the disposition to which the Spirit reveals God's will.

What do we read here? There were a number of men ministering to the Lord and fasting, and the Holy Ghost came and spoke to them. Some people understand this passage very much as they would in reference to a missionary committee of our day. We see there is an open field, we have had our missions in other fields, and we are going to get on to that field. We have virtually settled that, and we pray about it. But the position was a very different one in those former days. I doubt whether any of them thought of Europe, for later on even Paul himself tried to go back into Asia, till the night vision called him by the will of God. Look at those men. God had done wonders. He had extended the Church to Antioch, and He had given rich and large blessing. Now, here were these men ministering to the Lord, serving Him with prayer and fasting. What a deep conviction they have—"It must all come direct from Heaven. We are in fellowship with the risen Lord; we must have a close union with Him, and somehow He will let us know what He wants." And there they were, empty, ignorant, helpless, glad and joyful, but deeply humbled.

"O Lord," they seem to say, "we are thy servants, and in fasting and prayer we wait upon thee. What is thy will for us?"

Was it not the same with Peter? He was on the housetop, fasting and praying, and little did he think of the vision and the command to go to Caesarea. He was ignorant of what his work might be.

59

It is in hearts entirely surrendered to the Lord Jesus, in hearts separating themselves from the world, and even from ordinary religious exercises, and giving themselves up in intense prayer to look to their Lord—it is in such hearts that the heavenly will of God will be made manifest.

You know that word *fasting* occurs a second time (in the third verse), "They fasted and prayed." When you pray, you love to go into your closet, according to the command of Jesus, and shut the door. You shut out business and company and pleasure and anything that can distract, and you want to be alone with God. But in one way, even the material world follows you there. You must eat. These men wanted to shut themselves out from the influences of the material and the visible, and they fasted. What they ate was simply enough to supply the wants of nature, and in the intensity of their souls, they thought to give expression to their letting go of everything on earth in their fasting before God. Oh, may God give us that intensity of desire, that separation from everything, because we want to wait upon God, that the Holy Ghost may reveal to us God's blessed will.

The fourth thought—What is now the will of God, as the Holy Ghost reveals it? It is contained in one phrase: separation unto the Holy Ghost. That is the keynote of the message from Heaven.

> *"Separate Me Barnabas and Saul for the work whereunto I have called them. The work is mine, and I care for it, and I have chosen these men and called them, and I want you who represent the Church of Christ upon earth to set them apart unto me."*

Look at this heavenly message in its twofold aspect. The men were to be set apart to the Holy Ghost, and the Church was to do this separating work. The Holy Ghost could trust these men to do it in a right spirit. There they were abiding in fellowship with the heavenly, and the Holy Ghost could say to them, "Do the work of separating these men." And these were the men the Holy Ghost had prepared, and He could say of them, "Let them be separated unto me."

Here we come to the very root, to the very life of the need of Christian workers. The question is: What is needed that the power of God should rest upon us more mightily, that the blessing of God should be poured out more abundantly among those poor, wretched people and perishing sinners among whom we labor? And the answer from Heaven is:

"I want men separated unto the Holy Ghost."

What does that imply? You know that there are two spirits on Earth. Christ said, when He spoke about the Holy Spirit, "The world cannot receive Him." Paul said, "We have received not the spirit of the world, but the Spirit that is of God." That is the great want in every worker—the spirit of the world going out, and the Spirit of God coming in to take possession of the inner life and of the whole being.

I am sure there are workers who often cry to God for the Holy Spirit to come upon them as a Spirit of power for their work, and when they feel that measure of power, and get blessing, they thank God for it. But God wants something more and something higher. God wants us to seek for the Holy Spirit as a Spirit of power in our own heart and life, to conquer self and cast out sin, and to work the blessed and beautiful image of Jesus into us.

There is a difference between the power of the Spirit as a gift, and the power of the Spirit for the grace of a holy life. A man may often have a measure of the power of the Spirit, but if there be not a large measure of the Spirit as the Spirit of grace and holiness, the defect will be manifest in his work. He may be made the means of conversion, but he never will help people on to a higher standard of spiritual life, and when he passes away, a great deal of his work may pass away, too. But a man who is separated unto the Holy Ghost is a man who is given up to say:

"Father, let the Holy Ghost have full dominion over me, in my home, in my temper, in every word of my tongue, in every thought of my heart, in every feeling toward my fellow men; let the Holy Spirit have entire possession."

Is that what has been the longing and the covenant of your heart with your God—to be a man or a woman separated and given up unto the Holy Ghost? I pray you listen to the voice of Heaven. "Separate me," said the Holy Ghost. Yes, separated unto the Holy Ghost. May God grant that the Word may enter into the very depths of our being to search us, and if we discover that we have not come out from the world entirely, if God uncovers to us that the self-life, self-will, self-exaltation are there, let us humble ourselves before Him.

Man, woman, brother, sister, you are a worker separated unto the Holy Ghost. Is that true? Has that been your longing desire? Has that been your surrender? Has that been what you have expected through faith in the power of our risen and almighty Lord Jesus? If not, here is the call of faith, and here is the key of blessing—separated unto the Holy Ghost. God, write the word in our hearts!

I said the Holy Spirit spoke to that church as a church that was capable of doing that work. The Holy Spirit trusted them. God grant that our churches, our missionary societies, and our workers' unions, that all our directors and councils and committees may be filled with men and women who are fit for the work of separating workers unto the Holy Spirit. We can ask God for that, too.

Then comes my fifth thought—This holy partnership with the Holy Spirit in this work becomes a matter of consciousness and of action.

What did these men do? They set apart Paul and Barnabas, and then it is written of the two that they, being sent forth by the Holy Ghost, went down to Seleucia. Oh, what fellowship! The Holy Spirit in Heaven doing part of the work, men on Earth doing the other part. After the ordination of the men upon Earth, it is written in God's inspired Word that they were sent forth by the Holy Ghost.

And see how this partnership calls to new prayer and fasting. They had for a certain time been ministering to the Lord and fasting, perhaps days; and the Holy Spirit speaks, and they have to do the work and to enter into partnership, and at once they come together for more prayer and fasting. That is the spirit in which they obey the command of their Lord. And that teaches us that it is not only in the beginning of our Christian work, but all along, we need to have our strength in prayer. If there is one thought with regard to the Church of Jesus Christ

63

(which at times comes to me with overwhelming sorrow), if there is one thought in regard to my own life of which I am ashamed, if there is one thought of which I feel that the Church of Christ has not accepted and grasped, if there is one thought that makes me pray to God, "Oh, teach us by thy grace, new things"—it is the wonderful power that prayer is meant to have in the Kingdom. We have so little availed ourselves of it.

We have all read the expression of Christian in Bunyan's great work *Pilgrim's Progress*, when he found he had the key in his breast that should unlock the dungeon. We have the key that can unlock the dungeon of atheism and of heathendom. But, oh! We are far more occupied with our work than we are with prayer. We believe more in speaking to men than we believe in speaking to God. Learn from these men that the work which the Holy Ghost commands must call us to new fasting and prayer, to new separation from the spirit and the pleasures of the world, to new consecration to God and to His fellowship. Those men gave themselves up to fasting and prayer, and if in all our ordinary Christian work there were more prayer, there would be more blessing in our own inner life. If we felt and proved and testified to the world that our only strength lay in keeping every minute in contact with Christ, every minute allowing God to work in us—if that were our spirit, would not, by the grace of God, our lives be holier? Would not they be more abundantly fruitful?

I hardly know a more solemn warning in God's Word than that which we find in the third chapter of Galatians, where Paul asked:

"Having begun in the Spirit, are ye now made perfect by the flesh?"

64

Do you understand what that means? A terrible danger in Christian work, just as in a Christian life that is begun with much prayer, begun in the Holy Spirit, is that it may be gradually shunted off on to the lines of the flesh; and the word comes, "Having begun in the Spirit, are ye now made perfect by the flesh?" In the time of our first perplexity and helplessness, we prayed much to God. And God answered and blessed, our organization became perfected, and our band of workers became large, but gradually the organization and the work and the rush have so taken possession of us that the power of the Spirit, in which we began when we were a small company, has almost been lost. Oh, I pray you, note it well! It was with new prayer and fasting, with more prayer and fasting, that this company of disciples carried out the command of the Holy Ghost, "My soul, wait thou only upon God." That is our highest and most important work. The Holy Spirit comes in answer to believing prayer.

You know when the exalted Jesus had ascended to the throne, for ten days, the footstool of the throne was the place where His waiting disciples cried to Him. And that is the law of the Kingdom—the King upon the throne, the servants upon the footstool. May God find us there unceasingly!

Then comes the last thought—What a wonderful blessing comes when the Holy Ghost is allowed to lead and to direct the work, and when it is carried on in obedience to Him!

You know the story of the mission on which Barnabas and Saul were sent out. You know what power there was with them. The Holy Ghost sent them, and they went on from place to place with large blessing. The Holy Ghost was their leader further on. You recollect how it was by the Spirit that Paul was hindered from going again into Asia, and was led away over to Europe. Oh, the blessing that rested upon that little company of men, and upon their ministry unto the Lord!

I pray you, let us learn to believe that God has a blessing for us. The Holy Ghost, into whose hands God has put the work, has been called "the executive of the Holy Trinity." The Holy Ghost has not only power, but He has the Spirit of love. He is brooding over this dark world and every sphere of work in it, and He is willing to bless. And why is there not more blessing? There can be but one answer. We have not honored the Holy Ghost, as we should have done. Is there one who can say that that is not true? Is not every thoughtful heart ready to cry, "God, forgive me that I have not honored the Holy Spirit as I should have done, that I have grieved Him, that I have allowed self and the flesh and my own will to work where the Holy Ghost should have been honored! May God forgive me that I have allowed self and the flesh and the will actually to have the place that God wanted the Holy Ghost to have."

Oh, the sin is greater than we know! No wonder that there is so much feebleness and failure in the Church of Jesus Christ!

CHAPTER 4

Peter's Repentance

*And the Lord turned, and looked upon Peter. And
Peter remembered the word of the Lord, how he
had said unto him, Before the cock crow, thou
shalt deny me thrice. And Peter went out, and wept
bitterly. (Luke 22:61, 62)*

That was the turning point in the history of Peter.
Christ had said to him, "Thou canst not follow me
now." Peter was not in a fit state to follow Christ,
because he had not been brought to an end of himself; he
did not know himself, and he, therefore, could not follow
Christ. But when he went out and wept bitterly, then came
the great change. Christ previously said to him, "When
thou art converted, strengthen thy brethren." Here is the
point where Peter was converted from self to Christ.

I thank God for the story of Peter. I do not know a
man in the Bible who gives us greater comfort. When we
look at his character, so full of failures, and at what Christ
made him by the power of the Holy Ghost, there is hope
for every one of us. But remember, before Christ could fill
Peter with the Holy Spirit and make a new man of him, he
had to go out and weep bitterly; he had to be humbled. If
we want to understand this, I think there are four points
that we must look at. First, let us look at Peter, the devoted

disciple of Jesus; next, at Peter as he lived the life of self; then at Peter in his repentance; and last, at what Christ made of Peter by the Holy Spirit.

Peter the Devoted Disciple of Christ

Christ called Peter to forsake his nets, and follow Him. Peter did it at once, and he afterward could say rightly to the Lord:

"We have forsaken all and followed thee."

Peter was a man of absolute surrender; he gave up all to follow Jesus. Peter was also a man of ready obedience. You remember Christ said to him, "Launch out into the deep, and let down the net." Peter the fisherman knew there were no fish there, for they had been toiling all night and had caught nothing, but he said, "At thy word I will let down the net." He submitted to the word of Jesus. Further, he was a man of great faith. When he saw Christ walking on the sea, he said, "Lord, if it be thou, bid me come unto thee;" and at the voice of Christ, he stepped out of the boat and walked upon the water.

And Peter was a man of spiritual insight. When Christ asked the disciples, "Whom do ye say that I am?" Peter was able to answer, "Thou art the Christ, the Son of the living God." And Christ said, "Blessed art thou, Simon Barjona; for flesh and blood hath not revealed it unto thee, but my Father which is in heaven." And Christ spoke of him as the rock man, and of his having the keys of the Kingdom. Peter was a splendid man, a devoted disciple of Jesus, and if he were living nowadays, everyone would say that he was an advanced Christian. And yet, how much there was wanting in Peter!

Peter Living the Life of Self

You recollect that just after Christ had said to him, "Flesh and blood hath not revealed it unto thee, but my Father which is in heaven," Christ began to speak about His sufferings, and Peter dared to say, "Be it far from thee, Lord; this shall not be unto thee."

Then Christ had to say, "Get thee behind me, Satan; for thou savorest not the things that be of God, but those that be of men."

There was Peter in his self-will, trusting his own wisdom, and actually forbidding Christ to go and die. Where did that come from? Peter trusted in himself and his own thoughts about divine things. We see later on, more than once, that among the disciples, there were questions about who should be the greatest. Peter was one of them, and he thought he had a right to the very first place. He sought his own honor even above the others. The life of self was very strong in Peter. He had left his boats and his nets, but not his old self.

When Christ had spoken to him about His sufferings, and said, "Get thee behind me, Satan," He followed it up by saying, "If any man will come after me, let him deny himself, and take up his cross, and follow me." No man can follow Him unless he does that. Self must be utterly denied. What does that mean? When Peter denied Christ, we read that he said three times, "I do not know the man." In other words, "I have nothing to do with Him;

69

He and I are not friends; I deny having any connection with Him." Christ told Peter that he must deny self. Self must be ignored, and its every claim rejected. That is the root of true discipleship, but Peter did not understand it, and could not obey it.

And what happened? When the last night came, Christ said to him, "Before the cock crow twice thou shalt deny me thrice."

But with what self-confidence Peter said, "Though all should forsake thee, yet will not I. I am ready to go with thee, to prison and to death."

Peter meant it honestly, and Peter really intended to do it, but Peter did not know himself. He did not believe he was as bad as Jesus said he was.

We perhaps think of individual sins that come between God and us, but what are we to do with that self-life which is all unclean, our very nature? What are we to do with that flesh that is entirely under the power of sin? Deliverance from that is what we need. Peter did not know this, and therefore it was in his self-confidence that he went forth and denied his Lord.

Notice how Christ uses that word *deny* twice. He said to Peter the first time, "Deny self." He said to Peter the second time, "Thou wilt deny me." It is either of the two. There is no choice for us; we must either deny self or deny Christ. There are two great powers fighting each other—the self-nature in the power of sin, and Christ in the power of God. Either of these must rule within us.

Self made the devil. He was an angel of God, but he wanted to exalt self. He became a devil in hell. Self was the cause of the Fall of Man. Eve wanted something for herself, and so our first parents fell into all the wretchedness of sin. We, their children, have inherited an awful nature of sin.

Peter's Repentance

Peter denied his Lord thrice, and then the Lord looked upon him; and that look of Jesus broke the heart of Peter, and all at once there opened up before him the terrible sin that he had committed, the terrible failure that had come, and the depth into which he had fallen, and "Peter went out and wept bitterly."

Oh, who can tell what that repentance must have been? During the following hours of that night, and the next day, when he saw Christ crucified and buried, and the next day, the Sabbath—oh, in what hopeless despair and shame he must have spent that day!

"My Lord is gone, my hope is gone, and I denied my Lord. After that life of love, after that blessed fellowship of three years, I denied my Lord. God, have mercy upon me!"

I do not think we can realize into what a depth of humiliation Peter sank then. But that was the turning point and the change; and on the first day of the week, Christ was seen of Peter, and in the evening, He met him with the others. Later on at the Lake of Galilee, He asked him, "Lovest thou me?" until Peter was made sad by the thought that the Lord reminded him of having denied Him thrice; and said in sorrow, but in uprightness:

71

"Lord, thou knowest all things; thou knowest that I love thee."

Peter Transformed

Now Peter was prepared for deliverance from self, and that is my last thought. You know Christ took him with others to the footstool of the throne, and bade them wait there; and then on the Day of Pentecost, the Holy Spirit came, and Peter was a changed man. I do not want you to think only of the change in Peter, in that boldness, and that power, and that insight into the Scriptures, and that blessing with which he preached that day. Thank God for that. But there was something for Peter that was deeper and better. Peter's whole nature was changed. The work that Christ began in Peter when He looked upon him was perfected when he was filled with the Holy Ghost.

If you want to see that, read the First Epistle of Peter. You know wherein Peter's failings lay. When he said to Christ, in effect, "Thou never canst suffer; it cannot be"—it showed he had not a conception of what it was to pass through death into life. Christ said, "Deny thyself," and in spite of that, Peter denied his Lord. When Christ warned him, "Thou shalt deny me," and he insisted that he never would, Peter showed how little he understood what there was in himself. But when I read his epistle and hear him say, "If ye be reproached for the name of Christ, happy are ye, for the Spirit of God and of glory resteth upon you," then I say that it is not the old Peter, but that is the very Spirit of Christ breathing and speaking within him.

I read again, how he says, "Hereunto ye are called, to suffer, even as Christ suffered." I understand what a change had come over Peter. Instead of denying Christ, he found joy and pleasure in having self denied, crucified, and given up to the death. And therefore it is in the Acts we read that, when he was called before the council, he could boldly say, "We must obey God rather than men," and that he could return with the other disciples and rejoice that they were counted worthy to suffer for Christ's name.

You remember his self-exaltation; but now he has found out that "the ornament of a meek and quiet spirit is in the sight of God of great price." Again, he tells us to be "subject one to another, and be clothed with humility."

Dear friend, I beseech you, look at Peter utterly changed—the self-pleasing, the self-trusting, the self-seeking Peter, full of sin, continually getting into trouble, foolish and impetuous, but now filled with the Spirit and the life of Jesus. Christ had done it for him by the Holy Ghost.

And now, what is my object in having pointed thus very briefly to the story of Peter? That story must be the history of every believer who is ready to be made a blessing by God. That story is a prophecy of what everyone can receive from God in Heaven.

Now, let us just glance hurriedly at what these lessons teach us.

The first lesson is this—You may be a very earnest, godly, devoted believer, in whom the power of the flesh is yet very strong.

That is a very solemn truth. Peter, before he denied Christ, had cast out devils and had healed the sick; and yet the flesh had power, and the flesh had room in him. Oh, beloved, we want to realize that it is just because there is so much of that self-life in us that the power of God cannot work in us as mightily as God is willing that it should work. Do you realize that the great God is longing to double His blessing, to give tenfold blessing through us? But there is something hindering Him, and that something is a proof of nothing but the self-life. We talk about the pride of Peter, and the impetuosity of Peter, and the self-confidence of Peter. It is all rooted in that one word, self. Christ had said, "Deny self," and Peter had never understood and never obeyed; and every failing came out of that.

What a solemn thought, and what an urgent plea for us to cry: O God, do discover this to us, that none of us may be living the self-life! It has happened to many a one who had been a Christian for years, who had perhaps occupied a prominent position, that God found him out and taught him to find himself out, and he became utterly ashamed, falling down broken before God. Oh, the bitter shame and sorrow and pain and agony that came to him, until at last he found that there was deliverance! Peter went out and wept bitterly, and there may be many a godly one in whom the power of the flesh still rules.

And then my second lesson is—It is the work of our blessed Lord Jesus to discover the power of self.

How was it that Peter, the carnal Peter, self-willed Peter, Peter with the strong self-love ever became a man of Pentecost and the writer of his epistle? It was because Christ had him in His charge, and Christ watched over him, and Christ taught and blessed him. The warnings that Christ had given him were part of the training; and last of all, there came that look of love. In His suffering, Christ did not forget him, but turned round and looked upon him, and "Peter went out and wept bitterly." And the Christ who led Peter to Pentecost is waiting today to take charge of every heart that is willing to surrender itself to Him.

Are there not some people saying, "Ah! that is the mischief with me; it is always the self-life, and self-comfort, and self-consciousness, and self-pleasing, and self-will; how am I to get rid of it?"

My answer is: Only Christ Jesus can rid you of it; none else but Christ Jesus can give deliverance from the power of self. And what does He ask you to do? He asks that you should humble yourself before Him.

CHAPTER 5

Impossible With Man, Possible With God

And he said, The things which are impossible with men are possible with God. (Luke 18:27)

C hrist had said to the rich young ruler, "Sell all that thou hast ... and come, follow me." The young man went away sorrowful. Christ then turned to the disciples, and said, "How hardly shall they that have riches enter into the kingdom of God!" The disciples, we read, were greatly astonished, and answered, "If it is so difficult to enter the kingdom, who, then, can be saved?" And Christ gave this blessed answer:

"The things which are impossible with men are possible with God."

The text contains two thoughts—that in religion, in the question of salvation and of following Christ by a holy life, it is impossible for man to do it. And then alongside that is the thought—what is impossible with man is possible with God.

The two thoughts mark the two great lessons that man has to learn in the religious life. It often takes a long time to learn the first lesson: that in religion, man can do nothing, that salvation is impossible to man. And often a man learns that, and yet he does not learn the second lesson—what has been impossible to him is possible with God. Blessed is the man who learns both lessons! The learning of them marks stages in the Christian's life.

Man Cannot

The one stage is when a man is trying to do his utmost and fails, when a man tries to do better and fails again, when a man tries much more and always fails. And yet, very often he does not even then learn the lesson: With man, it is impossible to serve God and Christ. Peter spent three years in Christ's school, and he did not learn that it is impossible until he had denied his Lord and went out and wept bitterly. Then he learned it.

Just look for a moment at a man who is learning this lesson. At first, he fights against it; then, he submits to it, but reluctantly and in despair; at last, he accepts it willingly and rejoices in it. At the beginning of the Christian life, the young convert has no conception of this truth. He has been converted; he has the joy of the Lord in his heart; he begins to run the race and fight the battle; he is sure he can conquer, for he is earnest and honest, and God will help him. Yet, somehow, very soon he fails where he did not expect it, and sin gets the better of him. He is disappointed, but he thinks, "I was not watchful enough; I did not make my resolutions strong enough." And again he vows, and again he prays, and yet he fails. He thinks, "Am I not a regenerate man? Have I not the life of God within me?" And he thinks again, "Yes, and I have Christ to help me, I can live the holy life."

At a later period, he comes to another state of mind. He begins to see that such a life is impossible, but he does not accept it. Multitudes of Christians come to this point: "I cannot;" and then think God never expected them to do what they cannot do. If you tell them that God does expect it, it appears to them a mystery. A good many Christians are living a low life, a life of failure and of sin, instead of rest and victory, because they began to see, "I cannot; it is impossible." And yet they do not understand it fully, and so, under the impression, "I cannot," they give way to despair. They will do their best, but they never expect to get on very far.

But God leads His children on to a third stage: when a man understands that it is impossible, in its full truth, and yet at the same time says, "I must do it, and I will do it—it is impossible for man, and yet I must do it;" when the renewed will begins to exercise its whole power, and in intense longing and prayer, begins to cry to God, "Lord, what is the meaning of this? How am I to be freed from the power of sin?"

It is the state of the regenerate man in Romans 7. There you will find the Christian man trying his very utmost to live a holy life. God's law has been revealed to him as reaching down into the very depth of the desires of the heart, and the man can dare to say:

"I delight in the law of God after the inward man. To will what is good is present with me. My heart loves the law of God, and my will has chosen that law."

Can a man like that fail, with his heart full of delight in God's law and with his will determined to do what is right? Yes. That is what Romans 7 teaches us. There is something more needed. Not only must I delight in the Law of God after the inward man, and will what God wills, but also I need a divine omnipotence to work it in me. And that is what the Apostle Paul teaches in Philippians 2:13:

"It is God which worketh in you, both to will and to do."

Note the contrast. In Romans 7, the regenerate man says, "To will is present with me, but to do—I find I cannot do. I will, but I cannot perform." But in Philippians 2, you have a man who has been led on farther, a man who understands that when God has worked the renewed will, God will give the power to accomplish what that will desires. Let us receive this as the first great lesson in the spiritual life, "It is impossible for me, my God; let there be an end of the flesh and all its powers, an end of self, and let it be my glory to be helpless."

Praise God for the divine teaching that makes us helpless!

When you thought of absolute surrender to God, were you not brought to an end of yourself, and to feel that you could see how you actually could live as a man absolutely surrendered to God every moment of the day—at your table, in your house, in your business, in the midst of trials and temptations? I pray you learn the lesson now. If you felt you could not do it, you are on the right road, if you let yourselves be led. Accept that position, and maintain it before God, "My heart's desire and delight, O God, is absolute surrender, but I cannot perform it. It is impossible for me to live that life. It is beyond me." Fall down and learn that when you are utterly helpless, God will come to work in you not only to will, but also to do.

God Can

Now comes the second lesson: "The things which are impossible with men are possible with God."

I said a little while ago that there is many a man who has learned the lesson: It is impossible with men. And then he gives up in helpless despair, and lives a wretched Christian life without joy or strength or victory. And why? Because he does not humble himself to learn this other lesson: With God, all things are possible.

Your religious life is every day to be a proof that God works impossibilities; your religious life is to be a series of impossibilities made possible and actual by God's almighty power. That is what the Christian needs. He has an Almighty God that he worships, and he must learn to understand that he does not need a little of God's power, but he needs—with reverence be it said—the whole of God's omnipotence to keep him right, and to live like a Christian.

The whole of Christianity is a work of God's omnipotence. Look at the birth of Christ Jesus. That was a miracle of divine power, and it was said to Mary, "With God, nothing shall be impossible." It was the omnipotence of God. Look at Christ's resurrection. We are taught that it was according to the exceeding greatness of His mighty power that God raised Christ from the dead.

Every tree must grow on the root from which it springs. An oak tree three hundred years old grows all the time on the one root from which it had its beginning. Christianity had its beginning in the omnipotence of God, and in every soul it must have its continuance in that omnipotence. All the possibilities of the higher Christian life have their origin in a new apprehension of Christ's power to work all God's will in us.

I want to call upon you now to come and worship the Almighty God. Have you learned to do it? Have you learned to deal so closely with Almighty God that you know omnipotence is working in you? In outward appearance, there is often so little sign of it. The Apostle Paul said, "I was with you in weakness and in fear and in much trembling, and ... my preaching was ... in demonstration of the Spirit and of power." From the human side there was feebleness; from the divine side there was divine omnipotence. And that is true of every godly life; and if we would only learn that lesson better, and give a wholehearted, undivided surrender to it, we should learn what blessedness there is in dwelling every hour and every moment with Almighty God. Have you ever studied in the Bible the attribute of God's omnipotence? You know that it was God's omnipotence that created the world, and created light out of darkness, and man. But have you studied God's omnipotence in the works of redemption?

Look at Abraham. When God called him to be the father of that people out of whom Christ was to be born, God said to him, "I am God Almighty, walk before me, and be thou perfect." And God trained Abraham to trust Him as the omnipotent One. Abraham believed God in his going out to a land that he knew not, or his faith as a pilgrim amidst the thousands of Canaanites—his faith said, "This is my land." Abraham believed God in his faith in waiting twenty-five years for a son in his old age, against all hope. Abraham believed God in raising up of Isaac from the dead on Mount Moriah when he was going to sacrifice him. He was strong in faith, giving glory to God, because he believed that God who had promised was able to perform what He promised.

The cause of the weakness of your Christian life is that you want to work it out partly, and to let God help you. And that cannot be. You must come to be utterly helpless, to let God work, and God will work gloriously. We need this if we are indeed to be workers for God. I could go through Scripture and prove to you how Moses, when he led Israel out of Egypt; how Joshua, when he brought them into the land of Canaan; how all God's servants in the Old Testament counted upon the omnipotence of God to perform impossibilities. And this God lives today, and this God is the God of every child of His. And yet, some of us are wanting God to give us a little help while we do our best, instead of coming to understand what God wants, and to say, "I can do nothing. God must and will do all." Have you said, "In worship, in work, in sanctification, in obedience to God, I can do nothing of myself, and so my place is to worship the omnipotent God, and to believe that He will work in me every moment"? Oh, may God teach us this! Oh, that God would by His grace show you what a God you have, and to what a God you have entrusted yourself—an omnipotent God, willing with His whole omnipotence to place himself at the disposal of every child of His! Shall we not take the lesson of the Lord Jesus and say, "Amen; the things which are impossible with men are possible with God"?

Remember what we have said about Peter, his self-confidence, self-power, self-will, and how he came to deny his Lord. You feel, "Ah! there is the self-life, there is the flesh-life that rules in me!" And now, have you believed that there is deliverance from that? Have you believed that Almighty God is able so to reveal Christ in your heart, so as to let the Holy Spirit rule in you, that the self-life shall not have power or dominion over you? Have you coupled the two, and with tears of penitence and with deep humiliation and feebleness, cried out, "O God, it is impossible to me; man cannot do it, but glory to thy name, it is possible with God"? Have you claimed deliverance? Do it now. Put yourself afresh in absolute surrender into the hands of a God of infinite love; and as infinite as His love is His power to do it.

God Works in Man

But again, we came to the question of absolute surrender, and felt that that is the want in the Church of Jesus Christ, and that is why the Holy Ghost cannot fill us, and why we cannot live as people entirely separated unto the Holy Ghost; that is why the flesh and the self-life cannot be conquered. We have never understood what it is to be absolutely surrendered to God as Jesus was. I know that many earnestly and honestly say, "Amen, I accept the message of absolute surrender to God," and yet think, "Will that ever be mine? Can I count upon God to make me one of whom it shall be said in Heaven and on Earth and in hell, he lives in absolute surrender to God?" Brother, sister, "the things which are impossible with men are possible with God." Do believe that when He takes charge of you in Christ, it is possible for God to make you a man of absolute surrender. And God is able to maintain that. He is able to let you rise from bed every morning of the week with that blessed thought directly or indirectly, "I am in God's charge. My God is working out my life for me."

Some are weary of thinking about sanctification. You pray, you have longed and cried for it, and yet it appeared so far off! The holiness and humility of Jesus—you are so conscious of how distant it is. Beloved friends, the one doctrine of sanctification that is scriptural, real, and effectual is, "The things which are impossible with men are possible with God." God can sanctify men, and by His almighty and sanctifying power every moment, God can keep them. Oh, that we might get a step nearer to our God now! Oh, that the light of God might shine, and that we might know our God better!

I could go on to speak about the life of Christ in us—living like Christ, taking Christ as our Savior from sin, and as our life and strength. God in Heaven can reveal that in you. What does that prayer of the Apostle Paul say, "That he would grant you according to riches of his glory"—it is sure to be something very wonderful if it is according to the riches of His glory—"to be strengthened with might by his Spirit in the inner man"? Do you not see that it is an omnipotent God working by His omnipotence in the heart of His believing children, so that Christ can become an indwelling Savior? You have tried to grasp it and to seize it, you have tried to believe it, and it would not come. It was because you had not been brought to believe that "the things which are impossible with men are possible with God."

And so I trust that the word spoken about love may have brought many to see that we must have an inflowing of love in quite a new way. Our heart must be filled with life from above, from the Fountain of everlasting love, if it is going to overflow all the day. Then it will be just as natural for us to love our fellow men, as it is natural for the lamb to be gentle and the wolf to be cruel. Until I am brought to such a state that the more a man hates and speaks evil of me, and the more unlikable and unlovable a man is, the more I love him—until I am brought to such a state that the more the obstacles and hatred and ingratitude, the more the power of love can triumph in me—until I am brought to see that I am not saying, "It is impossible with men." But if you have been led to say, "This message has spoken to me about a love utterly beyond my power; it is absolutely impossible,"—then we can come to God and say, "It is possible with thee."

Some are crying to God for a great revival. I can say that that is the prayer of my heart unceasingly. Oh, if God would only revive His believing people! I cannot think in the first place of the unconverted formalists of the Church, or of the infidels and skeptics, or of all the wretched and perishing around me, my heart prays in the first place, "My God, revive thy Church and people." It is not for nothing that there are in thousands of hearts yearnings after holiness and consecration: it is a forerunner of God's power. God works to will and then He works to do. These yearnings are a witness and a proof that God has worked to will. Oh, let us in faith believe that the omnipotent God will work to do among His people more than we can ask. "Unto him," Paul said, "who is able to do exceeding abundantly above all that we ask or think.... unto him be glory." Let our hearts say that. Glory to God, the omnipotent One, who can do above what we dare to ask or think!

"The things which are impossible with men are possible with God." All around you there is a world of sin and sorrow, and the devil is there. But remember, Christ is on the throne, Christ is stronger, Christ has conquered, and Christ will conquer. But wait on God. My text casts us down, "The things, which are impossible with men;" but it ultimately lifts us up high—"are possible with God." Get linked to God. Adore and trust Him as the omnipotent One, not only for your own life, but also for all the souls that are entrusted to you. Never pray without adoring His omnipotence and saying, "Mighty God, I claim your almightiness." And the answer to the prayer will come, and like Abraham, you will become strong in faith, giving glory to God, because you account Him who has promised as being able to perform.

CHAPTER 6

"O Wretched Man That I Am"

O wretched man that I am! who shall deliver me
from the body of this death? I thank God through
Jesus Christ our Lord. (Romans 7:24, 25)

Y ou know the wonderful place that this text
has in Paul's epistle to the Romans. It stands
here at the end of the seventh chapter as the
gateway into the eighth. In the first sixteen verses
of the eighth chapter, the name of the Holy Spirit is found
sixteen times; you have there the description and promise
of the life that a child of God can live in the power of
the Holy Ghost. This begins in the second verse, "The
law of the Spirit of life in Christ Jesus hath made me free
from the law of sin and death." Paul goes on to speak of
the great privileges of the child of God, who is to be led
by the Spirit of God. The gateway into all this is in the
twenty-fourth verse of the seventh chapter, "O wretched
man that I am!"

There you have the words of a man who has come to
the end of himself. He has in the previous verses described
how he had struggled and wrestled in his own power to
obey the holy law of God, and had failed. But in answer to
his own question, he now finds the true answer and cries

out, "I thank God through Jesus Christ our Lord." He goes on to speak of the deliverance he has found.

I want to describe the path by which a man can be led out of the spirit of bondage, into the spirit of liberty. You know how distinctly it is said, "Ye have not received the spirit of bondage again to fear". We are continually warned that this is the great danger of the Christian life, to go again into bondage; and I want to describe the path by which a man can get out of bondage, into the glorious liberty of the children of God, and I want to describe the man himself.

First, these words are the language of a regenerate man; second, of an impotent man; third, of a wretched man; and fourth, of a man on the borders of complete liberty.

The Regenerate Man

There is much evidence of regeneration from the fourteenth verse of the chapter on to the twenty-third. "It is no more I that do it, but sin that dwelleth in me." That is the language of a regenerate man, a man who knows that his heart and nature have been renewed, and that sin is now a power in him that is not himself. "I delight in the law of the Lord after the inward man." That again is the language of a regenerate man. He dares to say when he does evil, "It is no more I that do it, but sin that dwelleth in me." It is of great importance to understand this.

In the first two great sections of this epistle, Paul deals with justification and sanctification. In dealing with justification, he lays the foundation of the doctrine in the teaching about sin, not in the singular sin, but in the plural, sins—the actual transgressions. In the second part of the fifth chapter, he begins to deal with sin, not as actual transgression, but as a power. Just imagine what a loss it would have been to us if we did not have this second half of the seventh chapter of the Epistle to the Romans, if Paul had omitted in his teaching this vital question of the sinfulness of the believer. We should have missed the question we all want answered as to sin in the believer. What is the answer? The regenerate man is one in whom the will has been renewed, one who can say, "I delight in the law of God after the inward man."

The Impotent Man

Here is the great mistake made by many Christian people: They think that when there is a renewed will, it is enough, but that is not the case. This regenerate man tells us, "I will to do what is good, but the power to perform I find not." How often people tell us that if you set yourself determinedly, you can perform what you will! But this man was as determined as any man can be, and yet he made the confession, "To will is present with me; but how to perform that which is good, I find not."

But, you ask, "Why does God make a regenerate man utter such a confession, with a right will, with a heart that longs to do good, and longs to do its very utmost to love God?"

Let us look at this question. What has God given us our will for? Had the angels who fell, in their own will, the strength to stand? Verily, no. The will of the creature is nothing but an empty vessel in which the power of God is to be made manifest. The creature must seek in God all that it is to be. You have it in the second chapter of the Epistle to the Philippians, and you have it here also, that God's work is to work in us both to will and to do of His good pleasure. Here is a man who appears to say, "God has not worked to do in me." But we are taught that God works both to will and to do. How is the apparent contradiction to be reconciled?

You will find that in this passage (Romans 7:6-25), neither the name of the Holy Spirit nor the name of Christ occurs even once. The man is wrestling and struggling to fulfill God's law. Instead of the Holy Spirit and of Christ, the Law is mentioned nearly twenty times. In this chapter, it shows a believer doing his very best to obey the Law of God with his regenerate will. Not only this, but you will find the little words, I, me, and my, occur more than forty times. It is the regenerate "I" in its impotence, seeking to obey the Law without being filled with the Spirit. This is the experience of almost every saint. After conversion, a man begins to do his best and fails, but if we are brought into the full light, we need fail no longer. Nor need we fail at all if we have received the Spirit in His fullness at conversion.

God allows failure that the regenerate man should be taught his own utter impotence. It is in the course of this struggle that there comes to us this sense of our utter sinfulness. It is God's way of dealing with us. He allows that man to strive to fulfill the Law, that, as he strives and wrestles, he may be brought to this, "I am a regenerate child of God, but I am utterly helpless to obey His Law." See what strong words are used all through the chapter to describe this condition, "I am carnal, sold under sin"; "I see another law in my members bringing me into captivity"; and last of all, "O wretched man that I am! who shall deliver me from the body of this death?" This believer who bows here in deep contrition is utterly unable to obey the Law of God.

The Wretched Man

Not only is the man who makes this confession a regenerate and impotent man, but he is also a wretched man. He is utterly unhappy and miserable; and what is it that makes him so utterly miserable? It is because God has given him a nature that loves himself. He is deeply wretched because he feels he is not obeying his God. He says, with brokenness of heart, "It is not I that do it, but I am under the awful power of sin, which is holding me down. It is I, and yet not I: alas! alas! it is myself; so closely am I bound up with it, and so closely is it intertwined with my very nature." Blessed be God when a man learns to say, "O wretched man that I am!" from the depth of his heart. He is on the way to the eighth chapter of Romans.

Many make this confession a pillow for sin. They say that Paul had to confess his weakness and helplessness in this way. Who are they that they should try to do better? So the call to holiness is quietly set aside. Would to God that every one of us had learned to say these words in the very spirit in which they are written here! When we hear sin spoken of as the abominable thing that God hates, do not many of us wince before the word? Would to God that all Christians who go on sinning and sinning would take this verse to heart. If ever you utter a sharp word, say, "O wretched man that I am!" And every time you lose your temper, kneel down and understand that it never was meant by God that this was to be the state in which His child should remain. Would to God that we would take this word into our daily life, and say it every time we are touched about our own honor, and every time we say sharp things, and every time we sin against the Lord God, and against the Lord Jesus Christ in His humility, and in His obedience, and in His self-sacrifice! Would to God that you could forget everything else, and cry out, "O wretched man that I am! who shall deliver me from the body of this death?"

Why should you say this whenever you commit sin? Because it is when a man is brought to this confession that deliverance is at hand.

And remember it was not only the sense of being impotent and taken captive that made him wretched, but it was above all the sense of sinning against his God. The law was doing its work, making sin exceeding sinful in his sight. The thought of continually grieving God became utterly unbearable—it was this that brought forth the piercing cry, "O wretched man!" As long as we talk and reason about our impotence and our failure, and only try to find out what Romans 7 means, it will profit us but little. But when once every sin gives new intensity to the sense of wretchedness, and we feel our whole state as one of not only helplessness, but actual exceeding sinfulness, we shall be pressed not only to ask, "Who shall deliver us?" but to cry, "I thank God through Jesus Christ, my Lord."

The Almost-Delivered Man

The man has tried to obey the beautiful law of God. He has loved it. He has wept over his sin. He has tried to conquer. He has tried to overcome fault after fault, but every time, he has ended in failure.

94

What did he mean by, *the body of this death*? Did he mean, *my body when I die*? Truthfully, no. In the eighth chapter, you have the answer to this question in the words, "If ye through the Spirit do mortify the deeds of the body, ye shall live." That is the body of death from which he is seeking deliverance.

And now he is on the brink of deliverance! In the twenty-third verse of the seventh chapter, we have the words, "I see another law in my members, warring against the law of my mind, and bringing me into captivity to the law of sin which is in my members." It is a captive that cries, "O wretched man that I am! Who shall deliver me from the body of this death?" He is a man who feels himself bound. But look to the contrast in the second verse of the eighth chapter:

> *"The law of the Spirit of life in Christ Jesus hath made me free from the law of sin and death."*

That is deliverance through Jesus Christ our Lord—liberty to the captive, which the Spirit brings. Can you keep captive any longer a man who has been made free by the "law of the Spirit of life in Christ Jesus"?

But you say, did not the regenerate man have the Spirit of Jesus when he spoke in the sixth chapter? Yes, but he did not know what the Holy Spirit could do for him.

God does not work by His Spirit as He works by a blind force in nature. He leads His people on as reasonable, intelligent beings, and, therefore, when He wants to give us that Holy Spirit whom He has promised, He brings us first to the end of self, to the conviction that though we have been striving to obey the Law, we have failed. When we have come to the end of that, then He shows us that in the Holy Spirit we have the power of obedience, the power of victory, and the power of real holiness.

God works to will, and He is ready to work to do, but, alas! many Christians misunderstand this. They think because they have the will, it is enough, and that now they are able to do. This is not so. The new will is a permanent gift, an attribute of the new nature. The power to do is not a permanent gift, but must be each moment received from the Holy Spirit. The man who is conscious of his own impotence as a believer will learn that by the Holy Spirit, he can live a holy life. This man is on the brink of that great deliverance; the way has been prepared for the glorious eighth chapter. I now ask this solemn question: Where are you living? Is it with you, "O wretched man that I am! who shall deliver me?" with now and then a little experience of the power of the Holy Spirit? or is it, "I thank God through Jesus Christ! The law of the Spirit hath set me free from the law of sin and of death"?

What the Holy Spirit does is to give the victory. "If ye through the Spirit do mortify the deeds of the flesh, ye shall live." The Holy Ghost does this—the third Person of the Godhead. When the heart is opened wide to receive Him, He comes in and reigns there, and mortifies the deeds of the body, day by day, hour by hour, and moment by moment.

I want to bring this to a point. Remember, dear friend, what we need is to come to decision and action. There are in Scripture two very different sorts of Christians. The Bible speaks in Romans, Corinthians, and Galatians about yielding to the flesh; and that is the life of tens of thousands of believers. All their lack of joy in the Holy

Ghost, and their lack of the liberty He gives, is just owing to the flesh. The Spirit is within them, but the flesh rules the life. To be led by the Spirit of God is what they need. Would to God that I could make every child of His realize what it means that the everlasting God has given His dear Son, Christ Jesus, to watch over you every day, and that what you have to do is to trust; and that the work of the Holy Spirit is to enable you. Every moment to remember Jesus, and to trust Him! The Spirit has come to keep the link with Him unbroken every moment. Praise God for the Holy Ghost! We are so accustomed to think of the Holy Spirit as a luxury, for special times, or for special ministers and men. But the Holy Spirit is necessary for every believer, every moment of the day. Praise God you have Him, and that He gives you the full experience of the deliverance in Christ, as He makes you free from the power of sin.

Who longs to have the power and the liberty of the Holy Spirit? Oh, brother, bow before God in one final cry of despair:

"O God, must I go on sinning this way forever? Who shall deliver me, O wretched man that I am, from the body of this death?"

Are you ready to sink before God in that cry and seek the power of Jesus to dwell and work in you? Are you ready to say, "I thank God through Jesus Christ"?

What good does it do that we go to church or attend conventions, that we study our Bibles and pray, unless our lives are filled with the Holy Spirit? That is what God wants, and nothing else will enable us to live a life of power and peace. You know that when a minister or parent is using the catechism, when a question is asked, an answer is expected. Alas! how many Christians are content with the question put here, "O wretched man that I am! Who shall deliver me from the body of this death?" but they never give the answer. Instead of answering, they are silent. Instead of saying, "I thank God through Jesus Christ our Lord," they are forever repeating the question without the answer. If you want the path to the full deliverance of Christ, and the liberty of the Spirit, the glorious liberty of the children of God, take it through the seventh chapter of Romans; and then say, "I thank God through Jesus Christ our Lord." Be not content to remain ever groaning, but say, "I, a wretched man, thank God, through Jesus Christ. Even though I do not see it all, I am going to praise God."

There is deliverance; there is the liberty of the Holy Spirit. The Kingdom of God is "joy in the Holy Ghost."

CHAPTER 7

Having Begun in the Spirit

*T*he words which I address to you are found in the Epistle to the Galatians, the third chapter, the third verse; let us read the second verse also, "This only would I learn of you, Received ye the Spirit by the works of the law, or by the hearing of faith? Are ye so foolish?" And then comes my text—"Having begun in the Spirit, are ye now made perfect by the flesh?"

When we speak of the quickening, the deepening, or the strengthening of the spiritual life, we are thinking of something that is feeble and wrong and sinful; and it is a great thing to take our place before God with the confession:

"O God, our spiritual life is not what it should be!"

May God work that into your heart, reader.

As we look round about at the Church, we see so many indications of feebleness, failure, sin, and shortcoming that we are compelled to ask: Why is it? Is there any necessity for the Church of Jesus Christ to be living in such a low state? Or is it actually possible that God's people should be living always in the joy and strength of their God?

Every believing heart must answer: It is possible.

Then comes the great question: Why is it, how is it to be accounted for, that God's Church as a whole is so feeble, and that the great majority of Christians are not living up to their privileges? There must be a reason for it. Has God not given Christ, His almighty Son, to be the Keeper of every believer, to make Christ an ever-present reality, and to impart and communicate to us all that we have in Christ? God has given His Son, and God has given His Spirit. How is it that believers do not live up to their privileges?

We find in more than one of the epistles a very solemn answer to that question. There are epistles, such as the first to the Thessalonians, where Paul writes to the Christians, in effect, "I want you to grow, to abound, to increase more and more." They were young, and there were things lacking in their faith, but their state was so far satisfactory, and gave him great joy, and he writes time after time, "I pray God that you may abound more and more; I write to you to increase more and more." But there are other epistles where he takes a very different tone, especially the epistles to the Corinthians and to the Galatians, and he tells them in many different ways what the one reason was, that they were not living as Christians ought to live; many were under the power of the flesh. My text is one example. He reminds them that by the preaching of faith they had received the Holy Spirit. He had preached Christ to them; they had accepted that Christ, and had received the Holy Spirit in power. But what happened? Having begun in the Spirit, they tried to perfect the work that the Spirit had begun in the flesh by their own effort. We find the same teaching in the Epistle to the Corinthians.

Now we have here a solemn discovery of what the great want is in the Church of Jesus Christ. God has called the Church of Jesus Christ to live in the power of the Holy

Spirit, and the Church is living for the most part in the power of human flesh, and of will and energy and effort apart from the Spirit of God. I do not doubt that this is the case with many individual believers. Oh, if God will use me to give you a message from Him, my one message will be this: "If the Church will return to acknowledge that the Holy Spirit is her strength and her help, and if the Church will return to give up everything, and wait upon God to be filled with the Spirit, her days of beauty and gladness will return, and we shall see the glory of God revealed among us." This is my message to every individual believer:

"Nothing will help you unless you come to understand that you must live every day under the power of the Holy Ghost."

God wants you to be a living vessel in whom the power of the Spirit is to be manifested every hour and every moment of your life, and God will enable you to be that.

Let us learn that this word to the Galatians teaches us some very simple thoughts. It shows us how (1) the beginning of the Christian life is receiving the Holy Spirit. It shows us (2) what great danger there is of forgetting that we are to live by the Spirit, and not live after the flesh. It shows us (3) what are the fruits and the proofs of our seeking perfection in the flesh. And then it suggests to us (4) the way of deliverance from this state.

Receiving the Holy Spirit

First of all, Paul says, "Having begun in the Spirit." Remember, the apostle not only preached justification by faith, but he preached something more. He preached this—the epistle is full of it—that justified men cannot live but by the Holy Spirit, and that therefore God gives to every justified man the Holy Spirit to seal him. The apostle says to them in effect more than once:

"How did you receive the Holy Spirit? Was it by the preaching of the law, or by the preaching of faith?"

He could point back to that time when there had been a mighty revival under his teaching. The power of God had been manifested, and the Galatians were compelled to confess:

"Yes, we have got the Holy Ghost: accepting Christ by faith, by faith we received the Holy Spirit."

Now, it is to be feared that there are many Christians who hardly know that when they believed, they received the Holy Ghost. A great many Christians can say, "I received pardon, and I received peace." But if you were to ask them, "Have you received the Holy Ghost?" they would hesitate, and many, if they were to say yes, would say it with hesitation; and they would tell you that they hardly knew what it was, since that time, to walk in the power of the Holy Spirit. Let us try to take hold of this great truth: The beginning of the true Christian life is to receive the Holy Ghost. And the work of every Christian minister is that which was the work of Paul—to remind his people that they received the Holy Ghost and must live according to His guidance and in His power.

If those Galatians who received the Holy Spirit in power were tempted to go astray by that terrible danger of perfecting in the flesh what had been begun in the Spirit, how much more danger do those Christians run who hardly ever know that they have received the Holy Spirit, or who, if they know it as a matter of belief, hardly ever think of it and hardly ever praise God for it?

Neglecting the Holy Spirit

But now look, in the second place, at the great danger.

Let's look at what shunting is on a railway. A locomotive with its train may be run in a certain direction, and the points at some place may not be properly opened or closed; unobservingly, it is shunted off to the right or to the left. And if that takes place, for instance, on a dark night, the train goes in the wrong direction, and the people might never know it until they have gone some distance.

And just so, God gives Christians the Holy Spirit with this intention, that every day all their life should be lived in the power of the Spirit. A man cannot live a godly life one hour unless it is by the power of the Holy Ghost. He may live a proper, consistent life—as people call it, an irreproachable life, a life of virtue and diligent service. But to live a life acceptable to God, in the enjoyment of God's salvation and God's love, to live and walk in the power of the new life—he cannot do so unless he is guided by the Holy Spirit every day and every hour.

But now listen to the danger. The Galatians received the Holy Ghost, but what was begun by the Spirit, they tried to perfect in the flesh. How? They fell back again under Judaizing teachers who told them they must be circumcised. They began to seek their religion in external observances. And so, Paul uses that expression about those teachers who had them circumcised, that "they sought to glory in their flesh."

You sometimes hear the expression, "religious flesh." What is meant by that? It is simply an expression made to give utterance to this thought: My human nature and my human will and my human effort can be very active in religion, and after being converted, and after receiving the Holy Ghost, I may begin in my own strength to try to serve God.

I may be very diligent and doing a great deal, and yet all the time it is more the work of human flesh than of God's Spirit. What a solemn thought, that man can, without noticing it, be shunted off from the line of the Holy Ghost on to the line of the flesh; that he can be most diligent and make great sacrifices, and yet it is all in the power of the human will! Ah, the great question for us to ask of God in self-examination is that we may be shown whether our religious life is lived more in the power of the flesh than in the power of the Holy Spirit. A man may be a preacher; he may work most diligently in his ministry; a man may be a Christian worker, and others may tell of him that he makes great sacrifices, and yet you can feel there is still something lacking in his life. You feel that he is not a spiritual man; there is no spirituality about his life. How many Christians there are about whom no one would ever think of saying, "What a spiritual man he is!" Ah! there is the weakness of the Church of Jesus Christ. It is all in that one word—flesh.

Now, the flesh may manifest itself in many ways. It may be manifested in fleshly wisdom. My mind may be most active about religion. I may preach or write or think or meditate, and delight in being occupied with things in God's Book and in God's Kingdom; and yet the power of the Holy Ghost may be markedly absent. I fear that if you take the preaching throughout the Church of Christ and ask why there is, alas! so little converting power in the preaching of the Word, why there is so much work and often so little result for eternity, why the Word has so little power to build up believers in holiness and in consecration—the answer will come: It is the absence of the power of the Holy Ghost. And why is this? There can be no other reason but that the flesh and human energy have taken the place that the Holy Ghost ought to have. That was true of the Galatians; it was true of the Corinthians. Paul said to them, "I cannot speak to you as to spiritual men; you ought to be spiritual men, but you are carnal." And you know how often in the course of his epistles he had to reprove and condemn them for strife and for divisions.

Lacking the Fruit of the Holy Spirit

A third thought: What are the proofs or indications that a church like the Galatians or a Christian is serving God in the power of the flesh—is perfecting in the flesh what was begun in the Spirit?

The answer is very easy. Religious self-effort always ends in sinful flesh. What was the state of those Galatians? Striving to be justified by the works of the Law. And yet they were quarreling and in danger of devouring one another. Count the expressions that the apostle uses to indicate their want of love, and you will find more than twelve—envy, jealousy, bitterness, strife, and all sorts of expressions. Read in the fourth and fifth chapters what he says about that. You see how they tried to serve God in their own strength, and they failed utterly. All this religious effort resulted in failure. The power of sin and the sinful flesh got the better of them, and their whole condition was one of the saddest that could be thought of.

This comes to us with unspeakable solemnity. There is a complaint everywhere in the Christian Church of the want of a high standard of integrity and godliness, even among the professing members of Christian churches. I remember a sermon, which I heard preached on commercial morality. And, oh, if we speak not only of the commercial morality or immorality, but also go into the homes of Christians, and if we think of the life to which God has called His children, and which He enables them to live by the Holy Ghost, and if we think of how much, nevertheless, there is of unlovingness and temper and sharpness and bitterness, and if we think how much there is very often of strife among the members of churches, and how much there is of envy and jealousy and sensitivity and pride—then we are compelled to say, "Where are marks of the presence of the Spirit of the Lamb of God?" Wanting, sadly wanting!

Many people speak of these things as though they were the natural result of our feebleness, and cannot well be helped. Many people speak of these things as sins, yet have given up the hope of conquering them. Many people speak of these things in the church around them, and do not see the least prospect of ever having the things changed. There is no prospect until there comes a radical change, until the Church of God begins to see that every sin in the believer comes from the flesh, from a fleshly life midst our religious activities, from a striving in self-effort to serve God. Until we learn to make confession, and until we begin to see, we must somehow or other get God's Spirit in power back to

His Church, we must fail. Where did the Church begin in Pentecost? There they began in the Spirit. But, alas, how the Church of the next century went off into the flesh! They thought to perfect the Church in the flesh.

Do not let us think, because the blessed Reformation restored the great doctrine of justification by faith, that the power of the Holy Spirit was then fully restored. If it is our faith that God is going to have mercy on His Church in these last ages, it will be because the doctrine and the truth about the Holy Spirit will not only be studied, but it will be sought after with a whole heart; and not only because that truth will be sought after, but because ministers and congregations will be found bowing before God in deep abasement with one cry: "We have grieved God's Spirit; we have tried to be Christian churches with as little as possible of God's Spirit; we have not sought to be churches filled with the Holy Ghost."

All the feebleness in the Church is owing to the refusal of the Church to obey its God.

And why is that so? I know your answer. You say, "We are too feeble and too helpless, and we try to obey, and we vow to obey, but somehow we fail."

Ah, yes, you fail because you do not accept the strength of God. God alone can work out His will in you. You cannot work out God's will, but His Holy Spirit can. Until the Church and the believers grasp this, and cease trying by human effort to do God's will, and wait upon the Holy Spirit to come with all His omnipotent and enabling power, the Church will never be what God wants her to be and is willing to make of her.

Yielding to the Holy Spirit

I come now to my last thought, which is in the form of this question: What is the way to restoration?

Beloved friend, the answer is simple and easy. If that train has been shunted off, there is nothing for it but to come back to the point at which it was led away. The Galatians had no other way in returning but to come back to where they had gone wrong, to come back from all religious effort in their own strength, and from seeking anything by their own work, and to yield themselves humbly to the Holy Spirit. There is no other way for us as individuals.

Is there any brother or sister whose heart is conscious? "Alas! my life knows but little of the power of the Holy Ghost." I come to you with God's message that you can have no conception of what your life would be in the power of the Holy Spirit. It is too high and too blessed and too wonderful, but I bring you the message that just as truly as the everlasting Son of God came to this world and wrought His wonderful works, that just as truly as on Calvary He died and wrought your redemption by His precious blood, so, just as truly, can the Holy Spirit come into your heart, that with His divine power He may sanctify you and enable you to do God's blessed will, and fill your heart with joy and with strength. But, alas! we have forgotten; we have grieved; we have dishonored the Holy Spirit, and He has not been able to do His work. But I bring you the message: The Father in Heaven loves to fill His children with His Holy Spirit. God longs to give each one individually, separately, the power of the Holy Spirit for daily life. The command comes to us individually, united. God wants us as His children to arise and place our sins before Him, and to call upon Him for mercy. Oh, are ye so foolish? Having begun in the Spirit, are ye perfecting in the flesh that which was begun in the Spirit? Let us bow in shame, and confess before God how our fleshly religion, our self-effort, and self-confidence have been the cause of every failure.

I have often been asked by young Christians, "Why is it that I fail so? I did so solemnly vow with my whole heart, and did desire to serve God. Why have I failed?"

To such I always give the one answer, "My dear friend, you are trying to do in your own strength what Christ alone can do in you."

And when they tell me, "I am sure I knew Christ alone could do it; I was not trusting in myself," my answer always is:

"You were trusting in yourself or you could not have failed. If you had trusted Christ, He could not fail."

Oh, this perfecting in the flesh that which was begun in the Spirit runs far deeper through us than we know. Let us ask God to discover to us that it is only when we are brought to utter shame and emptiness that we shall be prepared to receive the blessing that comes from on high.

And so, I come with these two questions. Are you living, beloved brother-minister—I ask it of every minister of the gospel—are you living under the power of the Holy Ghost? Are you living as an anointed, Spirit-filled man in your ministry and your life before God? O brethren, our place is an awful one. We have to show people what God will do for us, not in our words and teaching, but in our life. God help, us to do it!

I ask it of every member of Christ's Church and of every believer: Are you living a life under the power of the Holy Spirit day by day, or are you attempting to live without that? Remember, you cannot. Are you consecrated, given up to the Spirit to work in you and to live in you? Oh, come and confess every failure of temper, every failure of tongue however small, every failure owing to the absence of the Holy Spirit and the presence of the power of self. Are you consecrated, are you given up to the Holy Spirit?

If your answer is no, then I come with a second question: Are you willing to be consecrated? Are you willing to give up yourself to the power of the Holy Spirit?

You well know that the human side of consecration will not help you. I may consecrate myself a hundred times with all the intensity of my being, and that will not help me. What will help me is this—that God from Heaven accepts and seals the consecration.

And now are you willing to give yourselves up to the Holy Spirit? You can do it now. A great deal may still be dark and dim, and beyond what we understand, and you may feel nothing; but come. God alone can effect the change. God alone, who gave us the Holy Spirit, can restore the Holy Spirit in power into our life. God alone can "strengthen us with might by his Spirit in the inner man." And to every waiting heart that will make the sacrifice, give up everything, and give time to cry and pray to God, the answer will come. The blessing is not far off. Our God delights to help us. He will enable us to perfect, not in the flesh, but in the Spirit, what was begun in the Spirit.

CHAPTER 8

Kept by the Power of God

*T*he words from which I speak, you will find in 1 Peter 1:5. The third, fourth and fifth verses are, "Blessed be the God and Father of our Lord Jesus Christ, which ... hath begotten us again unto a lively hope by the resurrection of Jesus Christ from the dead, to an inheritance incorruptible ... reserved in heaven for you, who are kept by the power of God through faith unto salvation." The words of my text are, "Kept by the power of God through faith."

There we have two wonderful, blessed truths about the keeping by which a believer is kept unto salvation. One truth is, *Kept by the power of God*; and the other truth is, *Kept through faith*. We should look at the two sides—at God's side and His almighty power, offered to us to be our Keeper every moment of the day; and at the human side, we having nothing to do but in faith to let God do His keeping work. We are begotten again to an inheritance kept in Heaven for us; and we are kept here on Earth by the power of God. We see that there is a double keeping—the inheritance kept for me in Heaven, and I on Earth kept for the inheritance there.

Now, as to the first part of this keeping, there is no doubt and no question. God keeps the inheritance in Heaven very wonderfully and perfectly, and it is waiting there safely. And the same God keeps me for the inheritance. That is what I want to understand.

You know it is very foolish of a father to take great trouble to have an inheritance for his children, and to keep it for them, if he does not keep them for it. What would you think of a man spending his whole time and making every sacrifice to amass money? And as he gets his tens of thousands, you ask him why it is that he sacrifices himself so, and his answer is, "I want to leave my children a large inheritance, and I am keeping it for them." If you were then to hear that that man takes no trouble to educate his children, that he allows them to run upon the street wild, and to go on in paths of sin and ignorance and folly, what would you think of him? Would not you say, "Poor man! He is keeping an inheritance for his children, but he is not keeping or preparing his children for the inheritance?" And there are so many Christians who think, "My God is keeping the inheritance for me;" but they cannot believe, "My God is keeping me for that inheritance." The same power, the same love, the same God are doing the double work.

Now, I want to speak about a work God does upon us—keeping us for the inheritance. I have already said that we have two very simple truths: the one the divine side—we are kept by the power of God; the other, the human side—we are kept through faith.

Kept by the Power of God

Look at the divine side: Christians are kept by the power of God.

Keeping Includes All

Think, first of all, that this keeping is all-inclusive.

What is kept? You are kept. How much of you? The whole being. Does God keep one part of you and not another? No. Some people have an idea that this is a sort of vague, general keeping, and that God will keep them in such a way that when they die, they will get to Heaven. But they do not apply that word *kept* to everything in their being and nature. And yet, that is what God wants.

Here I have a watch. Suppose that this watch had been borrowed from a friend, and he said to me, "When you go to Europe, I will let you take it with you, but mind you keep it safely and bring it back."

And suppose I damaged the watch, and had the hands broken, and the face defaced, and some of the wheels and springs spoiled, and took it back in that condition, and handed it to my friend. He would say, "Ah, but I gave you that watch on condition that you would keep it."

"Have I not kept it? There is the watch."

"But I did not want you to keep it in that general way, so that you should bring me back only the shell of the watch, or the remains. I expected you to keep every part of it."

And so God does not want to keep us in this general way, so that at the last, somehow or other, we shall be saved as by fire, and just get into Heaven. But the keeping power and the love of God apply to every particular of our being.

Some people think God will keep them in spiritual things, but not in temporal things. This latter, they say, lies outside of His line. Now, God sends you to work in the world, but He did not say, "I must now leave you to go and earn your own money, and to get your livelihood for yourself." He knows you are not able to keep yourself. But God says, "My child, there is no work you are to do, and no business in which you are engaged, and not a cent which you are to spend, but I, your Father, will take that up into my keeping." God not only cares for the spiritual, but for the temporal also. The greater part of the life of many people must be spent, sometimes eight or nine or ten hours a day, amid the temptations and distractions of business, but God will care for you there. The keeping of God includes all.

Other people think, "Ah, in time of trial God keeps me, but in times of prosperity I do not need His keeping; then I forget Him and let Him go." Others, again, think the very opposite. They think, "In time of prosperity, when things are smooth and quiet, I am able to cling to God, but when heavy trials come, somehow or other my will rebels, and God does not keep me then."

Now, I bring you the message that in prosperity as in adversity, in the sunshine as in the dark, your God is ready to keep you all the time.

Then again, there are others who think of this keeping thus, "God will keep me from doing very great wickedness, but there are small sins I cannot expect God to keep me from. There is the sin of temper. I cannot expect God to conquer that."

When you hear of some man who has been tempted and gone astray or fallen into drunkenness or murder, you thank God for His keeping power.

"I might have done the same as that man," you say, "if God had not kept me." And you believe He kept you from drunkenness and murder.

And why do you not need to believe that God can keep you from outbreaks of temper? You thought that this was of less importance; you did not remember that the great commandment of the New Testament is—"Love one another as I have loved you." And when your temper and hasty judgment and sharp words came out, you sinned against the highest law—the law of God's love. And yet you say, "God will not, God cannot"—no, you will not say, "God cannot;" but you say, "God does not keep me from that." You perhaps say, "He can; but there is something in me that cannot attain to it, and which God does not take away."

I want to ask you, can believers live a holier life than is generally lived? Can believers experience the keeping power of God all the day, to keep them from sin? Can believers be kept in fellowship with God? And I bring you a message from the Word of God, in these words: *Kept by the power of God.* There is no qualifying clause to them. The meaning is that if you will entrust yourself entirely and absolutely to the omnipotence of God, He will delight to keep you.

Some people think that they never can get to the point that every word of their mouths should be to the glory of God. But this is something God wants of them; it is what God expects of them. God is willing to set a watch at the door of their mouth, and if God will do that, cannot He keep their tongue and their lips? He can; and that is what God is going to do for those who trust Him. God's keeping is all-inclusive, and let everyone who longs to live a holy life think out all their needs, and all their weaknesses, and all their shortcomings, and all their sins, and say deliberately, "Is there any sin that my God cannot keep me from?" And the heart will have to answer, "No; God can keep me from every sin."

Keeping Requires Power

Second, if you want to understand this keeping, remember that it is not only an all-inclusive keeping, but it is an almighty keeping.

I want to get that truth burned into my soul; I want to worship God until my whole heart is filled with the thought of His omnipotence. God is almighty, and the Almighty God offers himself to work in my heart, to do the work of keeping me; and I want to get linked with Omnipotence, or rather, linked to the Omnipotent One, to the living God, and to have my place in the hollow of His hand. You read the Psalms, and you think of the wonderful thoughts in many of the expressions that David uses; as, for instance, when he speaks about God being our God, our Fortress, our Refuge, our Strong Tower, our Strength, and our Salvation. David had very wonderful views of how the everlasting God is himself the hiding place of the believing soul, and of how He takes the believer and keeps him in the very hollow of His hand, in the secret of His pavilion, under the shadow of His wings, under His very feathers. And there David lived. And, oh, we who are the children of Pentecost, we who have known Christ and His blood and the Holy Ghost sent down from Heaven, why is it we know so little of what it is to walk tremblingly step by step with the Almighty God as our Keeper?

Have you ever thought that in every action of grace in your heart, you have the whole omnipotence of God engaged to bless you? When I come to a man and he bestows upon me a gift of money, I get it and go away with it. He has given me something of his; the rest he keeps for himself. But that is not the way with the power of God. God can part with nothing of His own power, and, therefore, I can experience the power and goodness of God only so far as I am in contact and fellowship with himself; and when I come into contact and fellowship with himself, I come into contact and fellowship with the whole omnipotence of God, and have the omnipotence of God to help me every day.

A son has, perhaps, a very rich father, and as the former is about to commence business, the father says, "You can have as much money as you want for your undertaking." All the father has is at the disposal of the son. And that is the way with God, your Almighty God. You can hardly take it in; you feel yourself to be such a little worm. His omnipotence was needed to keep a little worm! Yes, His omnipotence is needed to keep every little worm that lives in the dust, and also to keep the universe, and therefore His omnipotence is much more needed in keeping your soul and mine from the power of sin.

Oh, if you want to grow in grace, do learn to begin here. In all your judgings, meditations, thoughts, deeds, questionings, studies, and prayers, learn to be kept by your Almighty God. What is Almighty God not going to do for the child that trusts Him? The Bible says, "Above all that we can ask or think." You must learn to know and trust

Omnipotence, and then you will live as a Christian ought to live. How little we have learned to study God, and to understand that a godly life is a life full of God, a life that loves God and waits on Him, and trusts Him, and allows Him to bless it! We cannot do the will of God except by the power of God. God gives us the first experience of His power to prepare us to long for more, and to come and claim all that He can do. God help us to trust Him every day.

Keeping Is Continuous

This keeping is not only all-inclusive and omnipotent, but it is also continuous and unbroken.

People sometimes say, "For a week or a month God has kept me very wonderfully: I have lived in the light of His countenance, and I cannot say what joy I have had in fellowship with Him. He has blessed me in my work for others. He has given me souls, and at times, I felt as if I were carried heavenward on eagle's wings. But it did not continue. It was too good; it could not last." And some say, "It was necessary that I should fall to keep me humble." And others say, "I know it was my own fault, but somehow you cannot always live up in the heights."

Oh, beloved, why is it? Can there be any reason that the keeping of God should not be continuous and unbroken? Just think. All life is in unbroken continuity. If my life were stopped for half an hour, I would be dead, and my life would be gone. Life is a continuous thing, the life of God is the life of His Church, and the life of God is His almighty power working in us. And God comes to us as the Almighty One, and without any condition, He offers to be my Keeper, and His keeping means that day by day, moment by moment, God is going to keep us.

If I were to ask you the question, "Do you think God is able to keep you one day from actual transgression?" you would answer, "I not only know He is able to do it, but I think He has done it. There have been days in which He has kept my heart in His holy presence, when, though I have always had a sinful nature within me, He has kept me from conscious, actual transgression."

Now, if He can do that for an hour or a day, why not for two days? Oh! let us make God's omnipotence as revealed in His Word the measure of our expectations. Has God not said in His Word, "I, the Lord, do keep it, and will water it every moment"? What can that mean? Does "every moment" mean every moment? Did God promise of that vineyard or red wine that every moment He would water it so that the heat of the sun and the scorching wind might never dry it up? Yes. In South Africa, they sometimes make a graft, and above it, they tie a bottle of water, so that now and then there shall be a drop to saturate what they have put about it. And so, the moisture is kept there unceasingly until the graft has had time to stroke, and resist the heat of the sun.

Will our God, in His tenderhearted love toward us, not keep us every moment when He has promised to do so? Oh! if we once got hold of the thought: Our whole religious life is to be God's doing—"It is God that worketh in us to will and to do of his good pleasure"—when once we get faith to expect that from God, God will do all for us.

The keeping is to be continuous. Every morning God will meet you as you wake up. It is not a question: If I forgot to wake in the morning with the thought of Him, what will come of it? If you trust your waking to God, God will meet you in the morning as you wake with His divine sunshine and love, and He will give you the consciousness that through the day you have God to take charge of you continuously with His almighty power. And God will meet you the next day and every day; and never mind if, in the practice of fellowship, there comes failure sometimes. If you maintain your position and say, "Lord, I am going to expect you to do your utmost, and I am going to trust you day by day to keep me absolutely," your faith will grow stronger and stronger, and you will know the keeping power of God in unbrokenness.

Kept Through Faith

And now the other side—Believing. "Kept by the power of God through faith." How must we look at this faith?

Faith Implies Helplessness

Let me say, first of all, that this faith means utter impotence and helplessness before God.

At the bottom of all faith, there is a feeling of helplessness. If I have a bit of business to transact, perhaps to buy a house, the agent must do the work of getting the transfer of the property in my name, and making all the arrangements. I cannot do that work, and in trusting that agent, I confess I cannot do it. And so, faith always means helplessness. In many cases, it means I can do it with a great deal of trouble, but another can do it better. But in most cases, it is utter helplessness; another must do it for me. And that is the secret of the spiritual life. A man must learn to say, "I give up everything; I have tried and longed, and thought and prayed, but failure has come. God has blessed me and helped me, but still, in the long run, there has been so much of sin and sadness." What a change comes when a man is thus broken down into utter helplessness and self-despair, and says, "I can do nothing!"

Remember Paul. He was living a blessed life; he had been taken up into the third heaven, and then the thorn in the flesh came, "a messenger of Satan to buffet me." And what happened? Paul could not understand it, and he prayed to the Lord three times to take it away, but the Lord said, in effect:

"No; it is possible that you might exalt yourself, and therefore I have sent you this trial to keep you weak and humble."

And Paul then learned a lesson that he never forgot, and that was—to rejoice in his infirmities. He said that the weaker he was, the better it was for him, for when he was weak, he was strong in his Lord Christ.

Do you want to enter what people call "the higher life"? Then go a step lower down. I remember Dr. Boardman telling how that once he was invited by a gentleman to go to see some works where they made fine shot, and I believe the workmen did so by pouring down molten lead from a great height. This gentleman wanted to take Dr. Boardman up to the top of the tower to see how the work was done. The doctor came to the tower; he entered by the door and began going upstairs, but when he had gone a few steps, the gentleman called out, "That is the wrong way. You must come down this way. That stair is locked up."

The gentleman took him downstairs a good many steps, and there an elevator was ready to take him to the top; and he said, "I have learned a lesson that going down is often the best way to get up."

Ah, yes, God will have to bring us very low down; there will have to come upon us a sense of emptiness and despair and nothingness. It is when we sink down in utter helplessness that the everlasting God will reveal himself in His power, and that our hearts will learn to trust God alone.

What is it that keeps us from trusting Him perfectly?

Many say, "I believe what you say, but there is one difficulty. If my trust were perfect and always abiding, all would come right, for I know God will honor trust. But how am I to get that trust?"

My answer is, "By the death of self. The great hindrance to trust is self-effort. So long as you have your own wisdom and thoughts and strength, you cannot fully trust God. But when God breaks you down, when everything begins to grow dim before your eyes, and you see that you understand nothing, then God is coming nigh, and if you will bow down in nothingness and wait upon God, He will become all."

As long as we are something, God cannot be all, and His omnipotence cannot do its full work. That is the beginning of faith—utter despair of self, a ceasing from man and everything on earth, and finding our hope in God alone.

Faith Is Rest

And then we must understand that faith is rest.

In the beginning of the faith-life, faith is struggling, but as long as faith is struggling, faith has not attained its strength. When faith in its struggling gets to the end of itself, and just throws itself upon God and rests on Him, then comes joy and victory.

Perhaps I can make it plainer if I tell the story of how the Keswick Convention began. Canon Battersby was an evangelical clergyman of the Church of England for more than twenty years, a man of deep and tender godliness, but he had not the consciousness of rest and victory over sin, and often was deeply sad at the thought of stumbling and failure and sin. When he heard about the possibility of victory, he felt it was desirable, but it was as if he could not attain it. On one occasion, he heard an address on "Rest and Faith" from the story of the nobleman who came from Capernaum to Cana to ask Christ to heal his child. In the address, it was shown that the nobleman believed that Christ could help him in a general way, but he came to Jesus a good deal by way of an experiment. He hoped Christ would help him, but he had not any assurance of that help. But what happened? When Christ said to him, "Go thy way, for thy child liveth," that man believed the word that Jesus spoke; he rested in that word. He had no proof that his child was well again, and he had to walk back seven hours' journey to Capernaum. He walked back, and on the way met his servant, and got the first news that the child was well, that at one o'clock on the afternoon of the previous day, at the very time when Jesus spoke to him, the fever left the child. That father rested upon the word of Jesus and His work, and he went down to Capernaum and found his child well; and he praised God, and became with his whole house a believer and disciple of Jesus.

Oh, friends, that is faith! When God comes to me with the promise of His keeping, and I have nothing on Earth to trust in, I say to God, "Thy Word is enough; kept by the power of God." That is faith; that is rest.

When Canon Battersby heard that address, he went home that night, and in the darkness of the night, found rest. He rested on the word of Jesus. And the next morning, in the streets of Oxford, he said to a friend, "I have found it!" Then he went and told others, and asked that the Keswick Convention might be begun, and those at the convention with himself should testify simply what God had done.

It is a great thing when a man comes to rest on God's almighty power for every moment of his life, in prospect of temptations to temper and haste and anger and unlovingness and pride and sin. It is a great thing in prospect of these to enter into a covenant with the omnipotent Jehovah, not because of anything that any man says, or of anything that my heart feels, but on the strength of the Word of God, "Kept by the power of God through faith."

Oh, let us say to God that we are going to prove Him to the very uttermost. Let us say: "We ask you for nothing more than you can give, but we want nothing less." Let us say: "My God, let my life be a proof of what the omnipotent God can do. Let these be the two dispositions of our souls every day—deep helplessness, and simple, childlike rest."

Faith Needs Fellowship

That brings me to just one more thought in regard to faith—faith implies fellowship with God.

Many people want to take the Word and believe it, and they find they cannot believe it. Ah, no! you cannot separate God from His Word. No goodness or power can be received separate from God, and if you want to get into this life of godliness, you must take time for fellowship with God.

People sometimes tell me, "My life is one of such scurry and bustle that I have no time for fellowship with God." A dear missionary said to me, "People do not know how we missionaries are tempted. I get up at five o'clock in the morning, and there are the natives waiting for their orders for work. Then I have to go to the school and spend hours there; and then there is other work, and sixteen hours rush along, and I hardly get time to be alone with God."

Ah! there is the want. I pray you, remember two things. I have not told you to trust the omnipotence of God as a thing, and I have not told you to trust the Word of God as a written book, but I have told you to go to the God of omnipotence and the God of the Word. Deal with God as that nobleman dealt with the living Christ. Why was he able to believe the word that Christ spoke to him? Because in the very eyes and tones and voice of Jesus, the Son of God, he saw and heard something, which made him feel that he could trust Him. And that is what Christ can do for you and me. Do not try to stir and arouse faith from within. How often I have tried to do that, and made a fool of myself! You cannot stir up faith from the depths of your heart. Leave your heart, look into the face of Christ, and listen to what He tells you about how He will keep you. Look up into the face of your loving Father, and take time every day with Him, and begin a new life with the deep emptiness and poverty of a man who has nothing and wants to get everything from Him—with the deep relaxation of a man who rests on the living God, the omnipotent Jehovah. Try God and prove Him if He will not open the windows of Heaven and pour out a blessing that there shall not be room to receive it.

I close by asking if you are willing to experience to the very full the heavenly keeping for the heavenly inheritance. Robert Murray M'Cheyne says, somewhere, "Oh, God, make me as holy as a pardoned sinner can be made." And if that prayer is in your heart, come now, and let us enter into a covenant with the everlasting and omnipotent Jehovah afresh, and in great helplessness, but in great restfulness place ourselves in His hands. And then as we enter into our covenant, let us have the one prayer—that we may believe fully that the everlasting God is going to be our Companion, holding our hand every moment of the day; our Keeper, watching over us without a moment's interval; our Father, delighting to reveal himself in our souls always. He has the power to let the sunshine of His love be with us all the day. Do not be afraid because you have your business, that you cannot have God with you always. Learn the lesson that the natural sun shines upon you all the day, and you enjoy its light, and wherever you are you have the sun; God takes care that it shines upon you. And God will take care that His own divine light shines upon you, and that you shall abide in that light, if you will only trust Him for it. Let us trust God to do that with a great and entire trust.

Here is the omnipotence of God, and here is faith reaching out to the measure of that omnipotence. Shall we not say, "All that that omnipotence can do, I am going to trust my God for"? Are not the two sides of this heavenly life wonderful? God's omnipotence covers me, and my will in its littleness rests in that omnipotence, and rejoices in it!

> *Moment by moment, I'm kept in His love;*
> *Moment by moment, I've life from above;*
> *Looking to Jesus, the glory doth shine;*
> *Moment by moment, Oh, Lord, I am Thine!*

CHAPTER 9

Ye Are the Branches

An Address to Christian Workers

Everything depends on our being right ourselves in Christ. If I want good apples, I must have a good apple tree; and if I care for the health of the apple tree, the apple tree will give me good apples. And it is just so with our Christian life and work. If our life with Christ is right, all will come right. There may be the need of instruction and suggestion and help and training in the different departments of the work; all that has value. But in the long run, the greatest essential is to have the full life in Christ—in other words, to have Christ in us, working through us. I know how much there often is to disturb us, or to cause anxious questionings, but the Master has such a blessing for every one of us, and such perfect peace and rest, and such joy and strength, if we can only come into, and be kept in, the right attitude toward Him.

I will take my text from the parable of the Vine and the Branches, in John 15:5:

"I am the vine, ye are the branches." Especially these words, *"Ye are the branches."*

What a simple thing it is to be a branch, the branch of a tree, or the branch of a vine! The branch grows out of the vine or out of the tree, and there it lives and grows, and in due time, it bears fruit. It has no responsibility except just to receive sap and nourishment from the root and stem. And if we only by the Holy Spirit knew our relationship to Jesus Christ, our work would be changed into the brightest and most heavenly thing upon earth. Instead of there ever being soul-weariness or exhaustion, our work would be like a new experience, linking us to Jesus as nothing else can. For, alas! is it not often true that our work comes between us and Jesus? What folly! The very work that He has to do in me, and I for Him, I take up in such a way that it separates me from Christ. Many laborers in the vineyard have complained that they have too much work and no time for close communion with Jesus, that their usual work weakens their inclination for prayer, and that their too much interaction with men darkens the spiritual life. Sad thought, that the bearing of fruit should separate the branch from the vine! That must be because we have looked upon our work as something other than the branch bearing fruit. May God deliver us from every false thought about the Christian life.

Now, just a few thoughts about this blessed branch-life.

Absolute Dependence

In the first place, it is a life of absolute dependence. The branch has nothing; it just depends upon the vine for everything. Absolute dependence is one of the most solemn and precious of thoughts. A great German theologian wrote two large volumes some years ago to show that the whole of Calvin's theology is summed up in that one principle of absolute dependence upon God, and he was right. Another great writer has said that absolute, unalterable dependence upon God alone is the essence of the religion of angels, and should be that of men also. God is everything to the angels, and He is willing to be everything to the Christian, as well. If I can learn every moment of the day to depend upon God, everything will come right. You will get the higher life if you depend absolutely upon God.

Now, here we find it with the vine and the branches. Every vine you ever see, or every bunch of grapes that comes upon your table, let it remind you that the branch is absolutely dependent on the vine. The vine has to do the work, and the branch enjoys the fruit of it.

What has the vine to do? It has to do a great work. It has to send its roots out into the soil and hunt under the ground—the roots often extend a long way out—for nourishment, and to drink in the moisture. Put certain elements of manure in certain directions, and the vine sends its roots there, and then in its roots or stems it turns the moisture and manure into that special sap which is to make the fruit that is borne. The vine does the work, and the branch has just to receive from the vine the sap, which is changed into grapes. I have been told that at Hampton Court, London, there is a vine that sometimes bore a couple of thousand bunches of grapes, and people were astonished at its large growth and rich fruitage. Afterward it was discovered what was the cause of it. Not so very far away runs the River Thames, and the vine had stretched its roots away hundreds of yards under the ground, until it had come to the riverside. There in all the rich slime of the riverbed, it found rich nourishment, and obtained moisture. The roots had drawn the sap all that distance up and up into the vine, and as a result there was the abundant, rich harvest. The vine had the work to do, and the branches had just to depend upon the vine, and receive what it gave.

Is that literally true of my Lord Jesus? Must I understand that when I have to work, when I have to preach a sermon, or address a Bible class, or to go out and visit the poor, neglected ones, that all the responsibility of the work is on Christ?

That is exactly what Christ wants you to understand. Christ wants that in all your work, the very foundation should be the simple, blessed consciousness: Christ must care for all.

And how does He fulfill the trust of that dependence? He does it by sending down the Holy Spirit—not now and then only as a special gift, for remember the relationship between the vine and the branches is such that hourly, daily, unceasingly there is the living connection maintained. The sap does not flow for a time, and then stop, and then flow again, but from moment to moment, the sap flows from the vine to the branches. And just so, my Lord Jesus wants me to take that blessed position as a worker, and morning by morning and day by day and hour by hour and step by step, in every work I have, to go out just to abide before Him in the simple, utter helplessness of one who knows nothing, is nothing, and can do nothing. Oh, beloved workers, study that word, "nothing." You sometimes sing, "Oh, to be nothing, nothing," but have you really studied that word and prayed every day, and worshiped God in the light of it? Do you know the blessedness of that word, "nothing"?

If I am something, then God is not everything; but when I become nothing, God can become all, and the everlasting God in Christ can reveal himself fully. That is the higher life. We need to become nothing. Someone has well said that the seraphim and cherubim are flames of fire because they know they are nothing, and they allow God to put His fullness and His glory and brightness into them. Oh, become nothing in deep reality, and, as a worker, study only one thing—to become poorer and lower and more helpless, that Christ may work all in you.

Workers, here is your first lesson: learn to be nothing, learn to be helpless. The man who has something is not absolutely dependent; but the man who has nothing is absolutely dependent. Absolute dependence upon God is the secret of all power in work. The branch has nothing but what it gets from the vine, and you and I can have nothing but what we get from Jesus.

Deep Restfulness

Second, the life of the branch is not only a life of entire dependence, but of deep restfulness.

That little branch, if it could think and feel and speak—that branch away in Hampton Court vine, or on some of the million vines that we have in South Africa, in our sunny land—if we could have a little branch here today to talk to us, and if we could say, "Come, branch of the vine, I want to learn from you how I can be a true branch of the living Vine," what would it answer?

The little branch would whisper, "Man, I hear that you are wise, and I know that you can do a great many wonderful things. I know you have much strength and wisdom given to you, but I have one lesson for you. With all your hurry and effort in Christ's work, you never prosper. The first thing you need is to come and rest in your Lord Jesus. That is what I do. Since I grew out of that vine, I have spent years and years, and all I have done is just to rest in the vine. When the time of spring came, I had no anxious thought or care. The vine began to pour its sap into me, and to give the bud and leaf. And when the time of summer came, I had no care, and in the great heat, I trusted the vine to bring moisture to keep me fresh. And in the time of harvest, when the owner came to pluck the grapes, I had no care. If there was anything in the grapes that was not good, the owner never blamed the branch; the blame was always on the vine. And if you would be a true branch of Christ, the living Vine, just rest on Him. Let Christ bear the responsibility."

You say, "Won't that make me slothful?"

I tell you it will not. No one who learns to rest upon the living Christ can become slothful, for the closer your contact with Christ, the more of the Spirit of His zeal and love will be given unto you. But, oh, begin to work in the midst of your entire dependence by adding to that deep restfulness. A man sometimes tries and tries to be dependent upon Christ, but he worries himself about this absolute dependence; he tries and he cannot get it. But let him sink down into entire restfulness every day.

> *In Thy strong hand, I lay me down.*
> *So shall the work be done;*
> *For who can work so wondrously*
> *As the Almighty One?*

Worker, take your place every day at the feet of
Jesus, in the blessed peace and rest that come from the
knowledge—

I have no care; my cares are His!
I have no fear; He cares for all my fears.

Come, children of God, and understand that the Lord
Jesus wants to work through you. You complain of the
want of fervent love. It will come from Jesus. He will give
the divine love in your heart with which you can love
people. That is the meaning of the assurance, "The love of
God is shed abroad in our hearts by the Holy Spirit," and
of that other word, "The love of Christ constraineth us."
Christ can give you a fountain of love, so that you cannot
help loving the most wretched and the most ungrateful, or
those who have wearied you hitherto. Rest in Christ, who
can give wisdom and strength, and you do not know how
that restfulness will often prove to be the very best part of
your message. You plead with people and you argue, and
they get the idea, "There is a man arguing and striving
with me." They only feel, "Here are two men dealing with
each other." But if you will let the deep rest of God come
over you, the rest in Christ Jesus, the peace and rest and
holiness of Heaven, that restfulness will bring a blessing
to the heart, even more than the words you speak.

Much Fruitfulness

Third, the branch teaches a lesson of much
fruitfulness.

The Lord Jesus Christ repeated that word *fruit* often
in that parable. He spoke first of fruit, then of more fruit,

and then of much fruit. Yes, you are ordained not only to bear fruit, but to bear much fruit. "Herein is my Father glorified, that ye bear much fruit." In the first place, Christ said, "I am the Vine, and my Father is the Husbandman. My Father is the Husbandman who has charge of me and you." He who will watch over the connection between Christ and the branches is God; and it is in the power of God through Christ that we are to bear fruit.

Oh, Christians, you know this world is perishing for the want of workers. And it wants not only more workers—the workers are saying, some more earnestly than others, "We need not only more workers, but we need our workers to have a new power, a different life, that we workers should be able to bring more blessing." Children of God, I appeal to you. You know what trouble you take, say, in a case of sickness. You have a beloved friend apparently in danger of death, and nothing can refresh that friend so much as a few grapes, and they are out of season. But what trouble you will take to get the grapes that are to be the nourishment of this dying friend! And, oh, there are around you people who never go to church, and so many who go to church, but do not know Christ. And yet the heavenly grapes, the grapes of Eshcol, the grapes of the heavenly Vine are not to be had at any price, except as the child of God bears them out of his inner life in fellowship with Christ. Except the children of God are filled with the sap of the heavenly Vine, except they are filled with the Holy Spirit and the love of Jesus, they cannot bear much of the real heavenly grape. We all confess there is a great deal of work, a great deal of preaching and teaching and visiting, a great deal of machinery, a great deal of earnest effort of every kind; but there is not much manifestation of the power of God in it.

deal of work for Christ that is not the fruit of the heavenly
Vine. Do not seek for work only. Oh, study this question
of fruit bearing. It means the very life and the very power
and the very spirit and the very love within the heart of the
Son of God—it means the heavenly Vine himself coming
into your heart and mine.

You know there are different sorts of grapes, each
with a different name, and every vine provides exactly that
peculiar aroma and juice that gives the grape its particular
flavor and taste. Just so, there is in the heart of Christ Jesus
a life, a love, a Spirit, a blessing, and a power for men
that are entirely heavenly and divine, and that will come
down into our hearts. Stand in close connection with the
heavenly Vine and say:

*"Lord Jesus, nothing less than the sap that flows
through thyself, nothing less than the Spirit of thy
divine life is what we ask. Lord Jesus, I pray thee let
thy Spirit flow through me in all my work for thee."*

I tell you again that the sap of the heavenly Vine is
nothing but the Holy Spirit. The Holy Spirit is the life of
the heavenly Vine, and what you must get from Christ is
nothing less than a strong inflow of the Holy Spirit. You

need it exceedingly, and you want nothing more than that. Remember that. Do not expect Christ to give a bit of strength here, and a bit of blessing yonder, and a bit of help over there. As the vine does its work in giving its own peculiar sap to the branch, so expect Christ to give His own Holy Spirit into your heart, and then you will bear much fruit. And if you have only begun to bear fruit, and are listening to the word of Christ in the parable, "more fruit," "much fruit," remember that in order for you to bear more fruit, you just require more of Jesus in your life and heart.

We ministers of the gospel, how we are in danger of getting into a condition of work, work, work! And we pray over it, but the freshness and buoyancy and joy of the heavenly life are not always present. Let us seek to understand that the life of the branch is a life of much fruit, because it is a life rooted in Christ, the living, heavenly Vine.

Close Communion

Fourth, the life of the branch is a life of close communion.

Let us again ask: What has the branch to do? You know that precious, inexhaustible word that Christ used: *Abide*. Your life is to be an abiding life. And how is the abiding to be? It is to be just like the branch in the vine, abiding every minute of the day. There are the branches in close communion, in unbroken communion with the vine from January to December. And cannot I live every day—it is to me an almost terrible thing that we should ask the question—cannot I live in *abiding* communion with the heavenly Vine?

You say, "But I am so much occupied with other things."

You may have ten hours of hard work daily, during which your brain has to be occupied with temporal things; God orders it so. But the abiding work is the work of the heart, not of the brain, the work of the heart clinging to and resting in Jesus, a work in which the Holy Spirit links us to Christ Jesus. Oh, do believe that deeper down than the brain, deep down in the inner life, you can abide in Christ, so that every moment you are free, and the consciousness of this will come. "Blessed Jesus, I am still in thee."

If you will learn for a time to put aside other work and to get into this abiding contract with the heavenly Vine, you will find that fruit will come.

What is the application to our life of this abiding communion? What does it mean?

It means close fellowship with Christ in secret prayer. I am sure there are Christians who do long for the higher life, and who sometimes have a great blessing, and have at times found a great inflow of heavenly joy and a great outflow of heavenly gladness. And yet after a time, it has passed away. They have not understood that close, personal, actual communion with Christ is an absolute necessity for daily life. Take time to be alone with Christ. Nothing in Heaven or Earth can free you from the necessity for that, if you are to be happy and holy Christians.

Oh, how many Christians look upon it as a burden and a tax, and a duty, and a difficulty to be often alone with God! That is the great hindrance to our Christian life everywhere. We need more quiet fellowship with God, and

I tell you in the name of the heavenly Vine that you cannot be healthy branches, branches into which the heavenly sap can flow, unless you take plenty of time for communion with God. If you are not willing to sacrifice time to get alone with Him, and to give Him time every day to work in you, and to keep up the link of connection between you and himself, He cannot give you that blessing of His unbroken fellowship. Jesus Christ asks you to live in close communion with Him. Let every heart say, "O Christ, it is this I long for; it is this I choose." And He will gladly give it to you.

Absolute Surrender

Finally, the life of the branch is a life of absolute surrender.

This term, *absolute surrender*, is a great and solemn phrase, and I believe we do not understand its meaning. But the little branch preaches it.

"Have you anything to do, little branch, besides bearing grapes?"

"No, nothing."

"Are you fit for nothing?"

Fit for nothing! The Bible says that a bit of vine cannot even be used as a pen; it is fit for nothing but to be burned.

"And now, what do you understand, little branch, about your relationship to the vine?"

"My relationship is just this: I am utterly given up to the vine, and the vine can give me as much or as little sap as it chooses. Here I am at its disposal and the vine can do with me what it likes."

Oh, friends, we need this absolute surrender to the Lord Jesus Christ. The more I speak, the more I feel that this is one of the most difficult points to make clear, and one of the most important and needful points to explain—what this absolute surrender is. It is often an easy thing for a man or a number of men to come out and offer themselves up to God for entire consecration, and to say, "Lord, it is my desire to give up myself entirely to thee." That is of great value, and often brings very rich blessing. But the one question I ought to study quietly is, "What is meant by absolute surrender?"

It means that, as literally as Christ was given up entirely to God, I am given up entirely to Christ. Is that too strong? Some think so. Some think that never can be—that just as entirely and absolutely as Christ gave up His life to do nothing but seek the Father's pleasure, and depend on the Father absolutely and entirely, I am to do nothing but to seek the pleasure of Christ. But that is actually true. Christ Jesus came to breathe His own Spirit into us, to make us find our very highest happiness in living entirely for God, just as He did. Oh, beloved brethren, if that is the case, then I ought to say:

"Yes, as true as it is of that little branch of the vine, so true, by God's grace, I would have it to be of me. I would live day by day that Christ may be able to do with me what He will."

139

Ah! Here comes the terrible mistake that lies at the bottom of so much of our own religion. A man thinks, "I have my business and family duties, and my relationships as a citizen, and all this I cannot change. And now alongside all this, I am to take in religion and the service of God as something that will keep me from sin. God help me to perform my duties properly!"

This is not right. When Christ came, He came and bought the sinner with His blood. If there was a slave market here and I were to buy a slave, I should take that slave away to my own house from his old surroundings, and he would live at my house as my personal property, and I could order him about all the day. And if he were a faithful slave, he would live as having no will and no interests of his own, his one care being to promote the well-being and honor of his master. And in like manner I, who have been bought with the blood of Christ, have been bought to live every day with the one thought—How can I please my Master?

Oh, we find the Christian life so difficult because we seek for God's blessing while we live in our own will. We should be glad to live the Christian life according to our own liking. We make our own plans and choose our own work, and then we ask the Lord Jesus to come in and take care that sin shall not conquer us too much, and that we shall not go too far wrong; we ask Him to come in and give us so much of His blessing. But our relationship to Jesus ought to be such that we are entirely at His disposal, and every day come to Him humbly and straightforwardly and say:

"Lord, is there anything in me that is not according to thy will, that has not been ordered by thee, or that is not entirely given up to thee?"

Oh, if we would wait patiently, I tell you what the result would be. There would spring up a relationship between us and Christ that is so close and so tender that we should afterward be amazed at how we formerly could have lived with the idea, "I am surrendered to Christ." We should feel how far distant our interaction with Him had previously been, and that He can, and does indeed, come and take actual possession of us, and gives unbroken fellowship all the day. The branch calls us to absolute surrender.

I do not speak now so much about the giving up of sins. There are people who need that, people who have violent tempers, bad habits, and actual sins which they from time to time commit, and which they have never given up into the very bosom of the Lamb of God. I pray you, if you are branches of the living Vine, do not keep one sin back. I know there are a great many difficulties about this question of holiness. I know that not all think exactly the same with regard to it. That would be to me a matter of comparative indifference if I could see that all are honestly longing to be free from every sin. But I am afraid that unconsciously there are in hearts often compromises with the idea that we cannot be without sin; we must sin a little every day; we cannot help it. Oh, that people would actually cry to God, "Lord, do keep me from sin!" Give yourself utterly to Jesus, and ask Him to do His very utmost for you in keeping you from sin.

There is a great deal in our work, in our church and our surroundings that we found in the world when we were born into it. It has grown all around us, and we think that it is all right; it cannot be changed. We do not come to the Lord Jesus and ask Him about it. Oh, I advise you, Christians, bring everything into relationship with Jesus and say:

"Lord, everything in my life has to be in most complete harmony with my position as a branch of thee, the blessed Vine."

Let your surrender to Christ be absolute. I do not understand the phrase, surrender *fully*; it gets new meanings every now and then; it enlarges immensely from time to time. But I advise you to speak it out, "Absolute surrender to thee, O Christ, is what I have chosen." And Christ will show you what is not according to His mind, and lead you on to deeper and higher blessedness.

In conclusion, let me gather up all in one sentence. Christ Jesus said, "I am the Vine, ye are the branches." In other words, "I, the living One, who have so completely given myself to you, am the Vine. You cannot trust me too much. I am the Almighty Worker, full of a divine life and power." You are the branches of the Lord Jesus Christ. If there is in your heart the consciousness that you are not a strong, healthy, fruit-bearing branch, not closely linked with Jesus, not living in Him as you should be—then listen to Him say, "I am the Vine, I will receive you. I will draw you to myself. I will bless you. I will strengthen you. I will fill you with my Spirit. I, the Vine, have taken you to be my branches. I have given myself utterly to you. Children, give yourselves utterly to me. I have surrendered myself as God absolutely to you. I became man and died for you, that I might be entirely yours. Come and surrender yourselves entirely to be mine."

What shall our answer be? Oh, let it be a prayer from the depths of our heart, that the living Christ may take each one of us and link us close to himself. Let our prayer be that He, the living Vine, shall so link each of us to himself that we shall go away with our hearts singing, "He is my Vine, and I am His branches—I want nothing more—now I have the everlasting Vine." Then, when you get alone with Him, worship and adore Him, praise and trust Him, love Him, and wait for His love.

"Thou art my Vine, and I am thy branch. It is enough, my soul is satisfied."

Glory to His blessed name!

Study Guide

Biography of Andrew Murray

1. What can we be sure will happen when God places a desire within our hearts?

2. In which revival was Andrew Murray instrumental?

3. Where was Andrew Murray born?

4. What caused Andrew Murray to understand that greater power was available to the Church?

5. What preceded the Holy Spirit revival in Murray's church?

6. How many books did Murray write?

Chapter 1—Absolute Surrender

1. Have you absolutely surrendered everything to the Lord?

2. What is the condition of God's blessing?

3. How is absolute surrender accomplished in our lives?

4. How was Peter delivered and changed?

5. What should we do after we cast our self-life and flesh-life at the feet of Jesus?

Chapter 2—The Fruit of the Spirit is Love

1. What, according to Murray, is a chief reason why God cannot bless His church?

2. Why is love the fruit of the Spirit?

3. What is the only thing that can expel and conquer our selfishness?

4. How can we learn to love?

5. What is the reason that the Holy Spirit cannot come in power?

6. How is God's power demonstrated to the world?

7. What is the baptism of fire?

8. What is the role of love in the ministry of intercession?

9. Have you a lack of love to confess to God?

Chapter 3—Separated Unto the Holy Ghost

1. Who is the director of the work of God in the Earth?

2. What, according to Murray, should our first desire be?

3. How can a person know the will of God?

4. Is the longing of your heart to be a person who is separated unto the Holy Ghost?

5. Why is there so much feebleness and failure in the Church?

Chapter 4—Peter's Repentance

1. What was the turning point in Peter's history?

2. In what sense was Peter a man of absolute surrender?

3. What was it that changed Lucifer, an angel of God, into a demon of hell?

4. What was Murray's object in detailing the life of Peter?

Chapter 5—Impossible With Man, Possible With God

1. What does Romans 7 teach us?

2. What happens when we learn that we are utterly helpless?

3. Have you learned to worship an almighty God?

4. What is the cause of weakness in the Christian life?

5. Have you claimed deliverance for yourself?

Chapter 6—"O Wretched Man That I Am"

1. How is a person led out of the spirit of bondage into the spirit of liberty?

2. What does failure teach us?

3. Why should we say, "O wretched man that I am! Who shall deliver me from the body of this death?" every time we commit sin?

4. What makes us free from the law of sin and death?

5. Do you long to have the power and liberty of the Holy Spirit?

6. Are you ready to sink before God and seek the power of God to dwell and work in you?

7. Are you ready to say, "I thank God through Jesus Christ"?

Chapter 7—Having Begun in the Spirit

1. Having begun in the Spirit, are you now made perfect in the flesh?

2. Is it possible for God's people to always be living in the joy and strength of God?

3. Why do believers not live up to their potential and their privileges?

4. How does the flesh manifest itself?

5. Why is there so much feebleness in the Church?

6. Why do we sometimes fail?

7. What is the way to restoration?

8. Are you living under the power of the Holy Spirit?

9. Are you consecrated? Are you yielded to the Holy Spirit?

Chapter 8—Kept by the Power of God

1. What is the "double keeping" to which Andrew Murray refers?

2. Does God keep one part of you and not another?

3. Can a believer experience the keeping power of God all day?

4. Have you ever thought that in every action of grace in your heart, the whole omnipotence of God is engaged to bless you?

5. What will God not do for a child who trusts Him?

6. What feeling is at the bottom of all faith?

7. What was one lesson that Paul never forgot?

8. What keeps us from trusting God completely?

9. What does Murray mean by saying, "Faith is rest"?

Chapter 9—Ye Are the Branches

1. What does the vine do? What do the branches do?

2. What is the secret of all power in Christian work?

3. What does Murray mean by "abiding communion"?

4. What attitudes and attributes are characteristic of branches?

5. As a branch in the vine, what must you do?

Index

Pure Gold Classics

AN EXPANDING COLLECTION OF THE
BEST-LOVED CHRISTIAN CLASSICS OF ALL TIME.

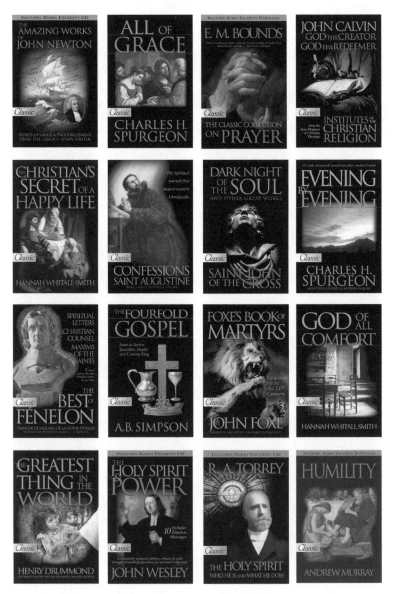

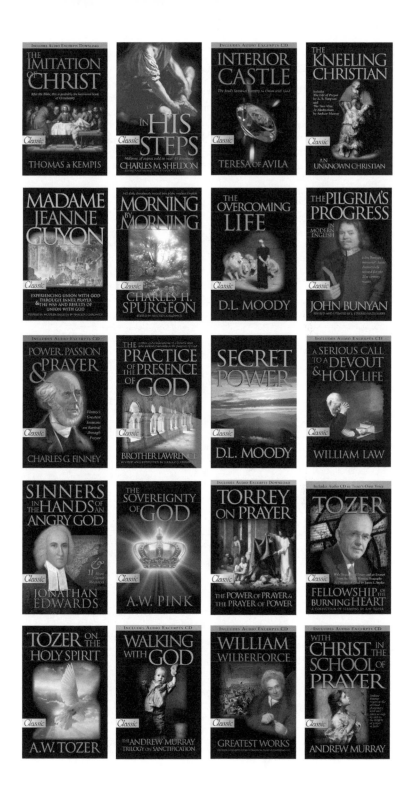

Includes Audio Excerpts Download
THE IMITATION OF CHRIST
After the Bible, this is possibly the best-loved book of Christianity.
Classic
THOMAS à KEMPIS

IN HIS STEPS
Millions of copies sold in over 45 languages
Classic
CHARLES M. SHELDON
REVISED AND REWRITTEN IN MODERN ENGLISH

Includes Audio Excerpts CD
INTERIOR CASTLE
The Jewel's Spiritual Journey to Union with God
Classic
TERESA OF AVILA

THE KNEELING CHRISTIAN
Includes The Life of Prayer by A. B. Simpson and The Two Vines: 31 Meditations by Andrew Murray
Classic
AN UNKNOWN CHRISTIAN

MADAME JEANNE GUYON
Classic
EXPERIENCING UNION WITH GOD THROUGH INNER PRAYER & THE WAY AND RESULTS OF UNION WITH GOD
REVISED IN MODERN ENGLISH BY HAROLD J. CHADWICK

365 daily devotionals revised from plain, modern English
MORNING BY MORNING
Classic
CHARLES H. SPURGEON
EDITED BY HAROLD J. CHADWICK

THE OVERCOMING LIFE
Classic
D.L. MOODY

THE PILGRIM'S PROGRESS
IN MODERN ENGLISH
John Bunyan's immortal classic dramatically revised for the 21st century reader.
Classic
JOHN BUNYAN
REVISED AND UPDATED BY L. EDWARD HAZELBAKER

Includes Audio Excerpts CD
POWER, PASSION & PRAYER
Finney's Greatest Sermons on Revival through Prayer
Classic
CHARLES G. FINNEY

THE PRACTICE OF THE PRESENCE OF GOD
Letters and conversations of a humble man who walked constantly in the presence of God
Classic
BROTHER LAWRENCE
REVISED AND REWRITTEN BY HAROLD J. CHADWICK

SECRET POWER
Classic
D.L. MOODY

Includes Audio Excerpts CD
A SERIOUS CALL TO A DEVOUT & HOLY LIFE
Classic
WILLIAM LAW

SINNERS IN THE HANDS OF AN ANGRY GOD
& 11 More Classic Messages
Classic
JONATHAN EDWARDS

THE SOVEREIGNTY OF GOD
Classic
A.W. PINK

Includes Audio Excerpts Download
TORREY ON PRAYER
Classic
THE POWER OF PRAYER & THE PRAYER OF POWER

Includes Audio CD in Tozer's Own Voice
TOZER
With Songs and Voices and an Excerpt from the Classic Biography by David Fant and James L. Snyder
Classic
FELLOWSHIP OF THE BURNING HEART
A COLLECTION OF SERMONS BY A.W. TOZER

TOZER ON THE HOLY SPIRIT
Classic
A.W. TOZER

Includes Audio Excerpts CD
WALKING WITH GOD
Classic
THE ANDREW MURRAY TRILOGY ON SANCTIFICATION

Includes Audio Excerpts CD
WILLIAM WILBERFORCE
Classic
GREATEST WORKS

Includes Audio Excerpts CD
WITH CHRIST IN THE SCHOOL OF PRAYER
Classic
ANDREW MURRAY